In Spite of It All

Stories Compiled by

ERICA WARREN

Table of Contents

Introduction

When you think of a champion, what usually comes to your mind? A picture of a boxer holding his glove above his head after winning a fight? An image of your favorite football team winning the Super Bowl and holding up a huge trophy? Those are a couple of the ideas that come to mind when we think of a champion, but I want to bring to your imagination a different kind of hero.

I want you to picture a woman scared, heartbroken, and heavily burdened. Picture her waking up every day, taking care of her kids, working on her job, and going out into the world looking like a million bucks. You would never suspect that she just cried her eyes out the night before. That's the kind of champion you're going to read about in the following pages of this book.

"In Spite of It All," is a collection of true-life testimonies from courageous women who have been through some hard trials in their lives. They were able to come out on top stronger, wiser, and better despite the circumstances that almost took them out of the game. If you're a person who loves to root for the underdog, if you're a person who gets satisfaction from hearing the story of a true overcomer, then you're really going to be touched by the women in this book.

Many of us have gone through situations in our lives where we felt like giving up. The reality of our perceived failure can become too much to bear. When we get stuck in this place of self-pity and self-loathing, we become easy access to the enemy. He loves to come in at our most vulnerable moments and rob us of our faith.

The heart-wrenching testimonies in this book will remind you that no matter how far off course you think you have gone, you're never too far gone for God. Whatever your situation is right now or however it may look at this moment, we want you to know that nothing that you have done or nothing that has happened to you can destroy the promises God has made to you. I pray that this book will give you courage and remind you that you're never alone.

I'm very honored to stand beside these ladies, sharing my story. The quote, "Thank God I don't look like what I've been through," can truly be said about this beautiful group of women. We know that this book will inspire you to keep going because "In Spite of It All, God's Got Your Back."

1

Nobody Sees Pain

Who would of thought that I would be staring death in the face, at the hands of my own husband? It was March 4, 2017, the day started out quite unusual. I had an eye appointment that day. Usually, my dad would go with me, but this day my husband and children went with me. My husband and I were having some issues and we were on the verge of separating in the coming months. Anyhow, we head out to the eye appointment.

I was having issues with my vision due to diabetic retinopathy. We arrived at the doctor's office, I signed in and we sat in the waiting room. The children were playing in the playroom. He sat there, his demeanor was strange and distant. As a matter of fact, he didn't even want to come with me to the appointment.

The doctor called my name and I went into the examination room to be seen. My pupils were dilated so they could look at the back of my eyes. I previously had surgery for a detached retina. The doctor was looking, he stated I needed to have another surgery to close a macular hole in the center of my vision, as I could see in my peripheral but not in the center.

My heart dropped as that was not the news I was expecting. So, the appointment ended, and my spirits were down. We leave to head back home. I was sad about the news I received so I mentioned to my husband he had been acting strange the whole appointment and wanted to know why. Immediately he was on defense mode and began cursing at me. Call me everything in the book with our children in the backseat, I then told him, he could start looking for his own place.

He then preceded to say that I could drive myself home, knowing I could not see the greatest as my eyes had been dilated and my vision was quite blurry. So, he pulls the car over and jumped out. Highly upset, I jumped over the arm rest into the driver's seat and drove off and left him standing there. I truly couldn't see so; I went back to get him. I turned around on the highway, driving in the wrong direction while using the emergency stop lane.

I pulled up to where he was, assuming he would get in the car and drive us home. I was so wrong. When I unlocked the door, he began hitting me in the head and pulling my hair. He then grabbed me by my jacket and was trying to throw me from my car into traffic. I said to myself, "Oh God, he is going to kill me." My kids were screaming and crying in the back.

I planted my feet in the floor as hard as I could grabbed hold of the steering wheel and arm rest to keep him from tossing me out into the busy highway. Then he grabbed my phone and threw it on the ground and cracked my screen so I couldn't call for help. He ran around to the passenger side of the car jumped in and pulled out this army looking knife and said, "Bitch I will kill you." My children are crying and screaming still. I didn't move as I thought he was really going to stab me. He stabbed the armrest.

Tears were streaming down my face while I thought my life was over. The police pulled up shortly thereafter as I was trying to dry my face, my kids were traumatized in the back. The officer got out, he came to the window and said, "You know you're driving the wrong way." then asked for my license and insurance. I guess by the look on my face and the children's faces, he asked if everything was okay?

I quickly said no and explained all that had just happened. The officer asked my husband to step out of the car, as he exited the vehicle, he threw the knife and his phone on the floor. He was quite boisterous with the officers and displayed he was quite angry. They wanted to arrest him, I told them not too, as my children had just seen enough. I just didn't want him back in the car with us. I was concerned about our safety.

The pain I felt emotionally and mentally was devastating. They told my husband he had to find him a way back home. I drove off with tears in my eyes, still my vision was quite blurry. By the grace of God and my children helping me by reading the signs, we made it safely back home. I drove straight to my father's house to tell him what happened.

I was in shock! The man I was married to for twelve years, tried to kill me in front of our kids. I thank GOD for life because I could have been gone. Sometimes I ask myself, what if he had been successful? What would he have done to our kids? I am forever grateful that we made it out this situation.

Needless to say, I got a divorce and have moved on with my life. Never in a million years did I think something of this magnitude would happen to me. I live this pain daily, as this wasn't the life I had pictured for my family. Never wanted to raise my children alone.

People look at me all the time, and they have no idea the pain and anguish I deal with daily. Pain is hidden in many ways. I laugh just to keep from crying. Just know that nobody sees pain, so whatever you're dealing with, you can get through it. With God all things are possible.

My relationship with God, and a strong prayer life gets me through the toughest of days. In spite of all I have gone through, I am making it and so can you. Hopefully, my story can inspire others to move past their pain and be the best version of themselves possible. So glad I don't look like all I have been through. I am making it and so can you!

Crisonda Watson, is a first-time author and entrepreneur, who has three businesses registered in Illinois. She's currently working as the Director of her own employment agency, Starrtemps Staffing. She also has a networking platform called "Blackronicles" and a former family childcare business called Starr Child Daycare.

She was born and raised in Erie, PA and currently resides in Joliet, IL. She is an amazing mother of two, her loving son Joshua and her loving daughter Cianna. She has always loved writing and want to inspire others to be the best version of themselves in whatever they do in life. Always remember nobody sees pain and you can overcome it all, with the help of God.

Follow me on Instagram CandiKane81
Facebook page Crisonda Watson

2

My Pit Experience

It was late one summer night when I was approached by a familiar spirit of rage, as my ex-husband approached. You know the feeling one gets in the pit of their stomach just before something happens. I was bathing my infant son but in the distance, I could tell that my now ex-husband was distressed as he approached the bathroom doorway. With anger in his eyes he replied, "Where in the hell have you been? You're going to make me take a knife and bust you upside the head."

Still calm, I replied, "What are you talking about? You know where I've been. I work and come home." I did not understand where this rage was coming from; to be threatened with physical harm, considering that I had grown up in a home with domestic violence. This was never the life that I wanted for myself or my children to witness, so I thought I was careful in explaining my do's and don'ts before marriage.

As I heard the drawers in the kitchen being forcefully opened and utensils banging around, I did the one thing that I knew, which was pray. I can remember how terrified I was for my son to witness an assault against his mother. I prayed with the door locked that God would intervene and help me because I knew I had done nothing wrong. I've never been so afraid that my life could end so swiftly by the hands of the man I married.

As I listened for him to go outside, I placed my son in his bedroom and went into the kitchen to find something to protect myself with. You see, I wasn't always calm natured and this situation could have easily taken me back to a pit that I had been long delivered from, a pit of anger and unforgiveness.

By this time, I had no more tears to shed because in my heart I wished for death to come. Growing up in domestic violence, my father would always come into my room as I pretended to sleep and said, "Baby girl I'm so sorry, I want you to know a man shouldn't treat a woman this way." I never quite understood why I was the one receiving the apology until I was in a similar pit.

As I walked outside with tears streaming from my eyes, I tossed away every knife, box cutter, and sharp utensil over the privacy fence into the field and asked God, "Why this was happening to me? Wasn't I a good wife and mother?" I couldn't find a reason that I was under an attack of this magnitude. My mother would always say that people either draw closer or push farther away from painful experiences.

Because of my painful childhood, I thought I had done everything to avoid anything similar to my past. My pit experience was the testing ground for my faith to rise up and take a stand for myself. I walked around in depression hoping someone would rescue me from the night-mare that I found myself in, but no one came to pull me out of this pit. This pit was the detour that changed my life.

After several months of break-ups and make-ups, I could not take it any longer and packed my bags to leave. Without warning, I arose early as my family was visiting from out of town and pleaded for them to take me away with them. I explained that my husband would not retaliate in their presence.

With my son in tow, I left everything behind and ran. I thought I had finally escaped the pit that was prepared for me. I arrived at my new location broken, battered and exhausted. I broke down in the shower as I began to shake uncontrollably and cry into the water to muffle the sound. I was so exhausted that I missed around six calls from my daughter in-forming me that she too was being harassed on her job by my husband.

What more could I do to escape from this torture and torment? I prayed, but it seemed like God wasn't hearing my prayers. I didn't want to die so what else could I do? My brother rushed home after being called by my daughter explaining what was happening back home and he was furious. He sat me down and with tears in his eyes, he said, "You got to go back home and fix this, you can't run from your problems."

I was suddenly filled with anxiety and tearfully thanked him for all the help, but I understood that I had to protect both of my children. The drive back home was silent as we passed through three states. We only stopped once. As I arrived home, all my things were unpacked, and I watched in horror as they drove away. "What do I do now?" swirled throughout my mind as I walked back into a house that no longer provided protection.

I wouldn't dare lie and tell you it was easy for me to pick up the pieces of my broken life, but in time, I found the courage to leave my marriage. The phone and text threats continued for several more months until I found myself in a pawn shop looking for a firearm. I remember thinking as the man explained the difference between various models, "What are you doing, this isn't you?"

I left with tears in my eyes and drove back home praying that God would help me because I didn't want to hurt anyone, but I didn't want anyone to hurt me either. I finally came to myself with the help of a life coach which helped me build the confidence to stand up for myself and take action. I remind myself daily that I owe it to myself to at least hear my inner voice in this lifetime. "Isn't it time to dream again, you can do it, I believe in you."

Nakita Terell Gridley-Radford-Malone-Haymer-Gonner-Haymer is a native of Arkansas. She is an educator, mentor, storyteller, and mother of two. Nakita's passion is to bring hope to young adults by sharing the detours of her life and the road to recovery. Nakita warmly shares her success with both her children, Aloria (21) and Ayden (5). She concludes by sharing, "If you don't learn to write your own story, someone else will."

3

Disobedience Can Cause Strife

"Future..."

I had no idea about the weight of this word. When I thought of it, I never imagined any struggles, failures, and disappointments. Only dreamed it would look like relief, relaxation, and pure beauty. "To become a nurse and make lots of money", is what I wrote in the "Future" section of my senior book in high school.

Thinking I had it all figured out, I became determined to go against every grain of the obstacles that came my way. I knew I had the drive and heart to succeed far beyond any doubt, but my impulsive decisions caused more problems than needed. Growing up, I felt like I had been waiting all my life. I could remember sitting outside waiting for my father to show up, it never happened or waiting on my mom to attend my school sports events, just to look out to find that she forgot again. "The wait was finally over", I told myself.

It was my final year of high school and waiting was no longer an option. I recall crying tears of joy at my graduation. I had made it through a tough journey but more importantly, I could start to live out the "future" I had adapted in my head. Waiting was no longer an option. It wasn't long before I attended college that I became pregnant with my first child.

Coming from a small town to a larger city was a big adjustment. Underestimating the path that life can take a person, I was in for much more than I had prepared for. The nightlife had me off focus and soon that pretty picture had just gotten real! I was in no way ready to be a mother. I reached out to my mentors to break the news about my pregnancy.

A part of me just knew that they would be disappointed, but they weren't. Both of them made me feel confident that I would survive this trial. The Taylor's always encouraged me throughout my high school years. They always gave me great advice, so breaking the news to them was a bit embarrassing for me. Shortly after Imani was born, a week later, in fact, I enrolled in school again.

I failed my last round, but I was ready to hop back in and give it another shot. The workload of school, a job, and a baby was a lot more than I could handle at the time. I flunked out again. After that, I fell into a dark place; victimizing myself and feeling hopeless about the dream that I wanted so bad to be my reality. Suppressing the feeling of being a failure through alcohol, marijuana, and sex.

It wasn't long after I had met my second child's father that I became pregnant. I wanted to go back to school but the academic advisor suggested that I do not attend until after I have the baby. I took her advice, tried again after the baby but failed again. It was like a never-ending cycle. This time I gave up on myself right in the middle of the program.

Stagnated and now with two children to support, nothing looked like what I pictured for myself; I was in a mess. A mess I did not know how to get out of, so back to the bottle I went. I went back to the blunts and back to having no degree. My whole life was in chaos. My relationships were struggling, my parenting became inconsistent, and I was clearly just surviving- far from living and my soul was not at peace.

I called my daughter's Godmother one night crying, fed up with the way my life was going. I told her that I wanted to move away; this wasn't for me anymore. During that conversation she said something that pierced my flesh. She said, "At some point you have to look at what you are doing and why you are attracting these situations into your life."

The truth never felt good. I never thought I could be the one to blame for all this bad luck. That night, I prayed harder than I had ever prayed before. The next day I was looking for answers. I decided to attend church that night. I was headed to another church but as I was driving, something in my gut pushed me to go to a church named "Revision." That night God led Pastor C to speak into my life.

He said, "God told me to tell you go and survey the land and wherever your feet lay ground, provisions are made." At that moment I heard a calm voice say "GO". I had never heard a voice like this before. The very next day I called up my sister and told her I was ready to go. I sold everything in my apartment and two weeks later I moved out of state terrified but obedient to the calmness in the voice that I heard.

Soon after I arrived at my new destination, I began to excel. I received a job within three weeks, an apartment in three months, and finally, I became a nurse within three years. After three years of trying to reach my goal, I finally did it. All I had to do was move out of Louisiana, so I thought. I was still mistakenly wrong.

In that same instance of me thinking that it was all ME, I heard a voice say, "Disobedience causes strife." I never talked to God about anything I was trying to do. It was right then that I understood the power of seeking God first. While God was waiting on me to put him first, my impulsive decision making and my determination to make things happen on my own kept me at a standstill for many years.

The most important lesson I took away from this was to always pray, wait on God to speak, and most importantly, be obedient and when He instructs you to go, that's the time to GO!

 **Latisha West,** is a thirty-three-year old Licensed Practical Nurse. She graduated from Tennessee College of Applied Technology and is currently practicing nursing in the field of corrections. She was born and raised in Louisiana but became a resident of Tennessee in 2014.

Her passion for the field of patient care is leading her to pursue an Associates Degree in Health Science at Jackson State Community College in Jackson, TN. She takes pride in being a mother to her four children, loves to read, write, and enjoys lots of laughter with family and friends.

She is very optimistic about her future and hopes to make a positive impact in people's lives along the way.

Follow her on Instagram@lwestisbak, email Lwest7069@gmail.com
Facebook Page @ Latisha West

4

My Year of Spiritual Warfare

No one could have told me that 2017 was not going to be my year. This was the year I would find a job, strengthen my relationship with God, lose weight, and be self-sufficient. I would no longer have to depend on my parent's financial support. I would no longer have a teeter tottering faith. I would no longer feel physically lethargic.

My life would no longer feel restrained. I had written the vision down, made it plain, and prayed over it with unwavering faith. However, I had no idea that over the course of the year, I would be tested in a way that would have me questioning my faith and my sanity. There were a series of events that occurred concurrently, which caused me to sink low, so quickly, and I did not realize how far removed I was from the jovial, faith-filled woman who entered the beginning of the year.

I can honestly say the first two months of the year were not bad at all, but yielded no change, and I was fine with knowing I had several more months for a change to come. Change did show up, but it showed up in the form of pain and dysfunction. The beginning of March until mid-June were the hardest months of my life. My mother had a major surgery, which placed me in the role of caretaker.

I had to see to my twelve-year-old and one-year old nephews while my niece was away attending college. My mother decided to renovate our entire house during her recovery stage. Combining surgery recovery and a renovation was not a great idea. We had no outside help during this period of time with the house and my mother's recovery, and I started to feel some type of way about it.

The next thing that happened really caused me major disappointment and set the tone for the dynamics of my family for the next few months. My family dysfunction was an indication that the enemy had planted seeds of discord, and some of those seeds had rooted themselves and sprouted in different areas. One spring evening as a family member spiraled out of control and physically assaulted me and my parents, a seed of pain and bitterness was planted in my spirit.

Directly after this situation, other family members started to act out of character. The enemy continued to work throughout my family and plant seeds of distrust, lies, anger, contention, and manipulation. Family members who we were extremely close to, literally did a "Dr. Jekyll and Mr. Hyde" transformation that was mind boggling. Communication was filled with accusations and blatant disrespect. This led to the beginning of me questioning my faith in God and illogically questioning God's providence.

I was totally blindsided by everything. I began to wonder if this was how Joseph in the Bible felt when his brothers turned against him and sold him into slavery. I was an unwilling participant in something I never signed up for and would never sign up for. My faith was at an all-time low, and I was so conflicted by everything, which turned into another facet of conflict. Subconsciously, I erected a barrier between me and God, all while ruminating in emotional disbelief about His absence.

By mentally and verbally rehearsing every day the spiteful actions and words directed towards me, I became emotionally and spiritually constipated, further cementing the wall I built between God and myself. My sanity was in question because I could not halt mentally repeating every word, every action directed towards me that was unimaginable from what I knew beforehand.

There was a blockage that hindered the effectiveness of my faith. My emotions were restricted by the hardening of my heart. I could not pray coherently. I could not cry. I could not laugh. I was spiritually impassable and even straining to successfully produce any reaction. My life miserably echoed an agreement with discord, and I honestly entertained selfish thoughts of someone dying to bring back the normalcy I was familiar with. Yet, nothing was normal, and the devil was rejoicing.

All of the things I envisioned for my life for 2017 was a forgone conclusion. I did not care if any personal goals were accomplished (i.e. financial independence and self-sufficiency). I easily lost weight due to the stress of the situation, and my faith was so rundown. Despite my incomplete yet desperate and incoherent prayers, God sent reinforcements.

My cousin issued an invitation in the month of May for a family trip at the end of June to Gatlinburg, Tennessee. This was a lifeline I didn't know I needed, we needed. Despite renovations, my mother's recovery, and family discord, we gladly traveled those nine plus hours from Louisiana to Tennessee. Even though we were experiencing something new, I was still fraught in my spirit and emotions.

Regardless of my inner struggle, God revealed something to me during our family trip which pushed me towards breakthrough after returning from Tennessee. I never thought I had the ability to drive to an unacquainted place with confidence. I noticed the ambition within me to conquer the unfamiliar. This determination produced a resolute outlook that everything prior to this trip was unfamiliar as well.

However, just like I had the determination to conquer the unfamiliar for a family vacation, I could have the same determination to conquer the unrest in my spirit. The solution to end the war in my spirit was simple: fasting and praying. I spent three days fasting and praying for my family and myself. A peace that I knew only came from God fell upon me and broke the chains of despair, confusion, and pain.

No, my situation did not improve immediately, it actually worsened in some areas, but God trained me to have peace in the midst of the storm. In my darkest hour, God strengthened my character and produced a persevering spirit. It all seemed unfair in the beginning, but He worked all things together for my good.

Latoya Garrett, was born and raised in a small town in Louisiana. She has a BA in Psychology from Southeastern Louisiana University, and currently works for the Louisiana Department of Children & Family Services. Latoya is an avid reader, as well as, a lover of crime TV shows.

She enjoys spending time with family, watching good movies, strawberry cheesecake, and putting a smile on others' faces. She is a blogger, certified wedding planner, and occasional background actor. You can read her blog at www.inspirationbytoyadenae.com and follow her on Instagram @inspirationbytoyadenae

Facebook page @authorlatoyagarrett. You can contact her email at inspirationbytoyadenae@gmail.com.

5

Finding Strength Within My Broken Heart

I went through a disastrous breakup in 2013. It mentally and physically broke me. I was a hopeless romantic, so I was in love with the idea of being in love. The first year of the relationship was perfect. The "good morning" text messages and the surprise gifts would brighten up my day.

This guy could do no wrong in my eyes. The anger or the attitude he would have from time to time didn't matter because the love outweighed it all. By the second year of the relationship, I was being mentally and physically abused. I can say that I wasn't the statistic that they bestow on Black families. I grew up in a home where I had both my parents who have been married for thirty-five years.

Why would this girl, who had the ideal marriage in front of her settle for an abusive relationship you ask?

Low self-esteem?

Pride?

Mental issues?

Not feeling worthy?

At the time I was a young woman who didn't feel pretty and had issues with low self-esteem. My boyfriend, at the time, knew all the right words to get me to stay. One fight, one push, and one hit would eventually leave me crying and him leaving in my car for hours and then coming back to apologize.

I was hurt, ashamed, and embarrassed. How in the world did I get myself into this? I began to pray to God to remove me from this situation and I promised I wouldn't go back. I broke up with him for about two weeks, then the loneliness at night began to set into place again. It's crazy because men know when to reach out to you.

All it took was the apology and how much he loves me, and it will never happen again for me to go back into the same environment. I went back into the relationship and of course he was being "the perfect guy." I remember I had an interview for a job, and I was in the interview for over an hour. I was so happy to walk out and to see he stayed and waited the whole time. I got to the car and saw him hang up the phone fast; I instantly knew it was another woman.

I grabbed the phone out of his hand only to start another fight. The fight was so intense that when I look back now, I'm shocked to say that I was even in a situation where I was fighting a man. When we finally made it back to the house, he pulled me out of the car, into the mud, and repeatedly hit me in the face until I felt my mouth fill with blood. He then went into the house and began throwing all my clothes at me.

I mean he was literally throwing out my shirts, panties, and bras. Anything that I might have left he was throwing at me, as if I meant nothing to him. To be honest, that's exactly how I felt- as if I was nothing. I allowed myself to go back to this situation so why did I deserve anything better than this? I wanted to die. I remember screaming and telling him to stop because I felt as if I couldn't breathe.

This was the moment it hit me- I needed to get my stuff and never look back. I grabbed my clothes and the little dignity I had left and went home. Why did it take me three years to realize that the problem wasn't in the man or my family, but it was me. Everyone has a breaking point and after three years, I had reached mine. I had to find myself because I was lost. I would look in the mirror and not even see myself anymore.

I knew that I had to find the woman within me. This wasn't an easy process, but I knew it would be worth it. I remember asking God for forgiveness for losing sight and putting a man before him. My grandmother would tell me that once I asked God for forgiveness, I had to walk away knowing that God has forgiven me without any questions. I changed my number so he wouldn't be able to contact me at all.

I deleted him and his family from my social media. I made sure I took the steps to remove any communication between us. The process of moving on is hard but the reward is greater. I prayed for clarity and direction. I would go to church and Bible study, but there were still days I didn't feel like getting out of the bed.

There were some really bad days and moments that I would try to get in touch with him, but then I would look in the mirror and see the bruises that were beginning to heal. I didn't want to keep putting on makeup to hide bruises and scars; so I refused to go back. God gave me the strength I needed to move on and to not look back.

I went back to school and received my Associates Degree and I graduated this past May with my Bachelor's Degree in Communications. I decided to follow my dream and become an author. I want to let you know that each day that you wake up is God letting you know that you have a purpose and your story is still being written. I look back and I'm amazed at the woman I have become.

I know that you're reading this and having doubts on whether or not you're ready to make that move and I'm telling you now that this is your confirmation to leave that man and trust God. Make the first step of loving yourself and being strong enough to leave. I smile without worrying about a man or the future because God is within me. I pray that you take the first step to healing yourself, loving yourself, and following your dreams.

Shronda Beeks, was born and raised in Mississippi. She realized at a young age that writing was her passion. Shronda is a single mother to a son who she adores and is big on family values. She has a Bachelor's Degree in Communications.

Shronda is a woman of God who looks to inspire and encourage women to find the good within themselves. She uses writing to help encourage others to step out on faith and to follow their dreams. When she's not writing, she is reading, blogging, and expanding her horizons in the world of writing. She will be releasing more books soon.

Facebook: Shronda Beeks
Instagram:Rhondathewriter

6

My Hurt Was for My Good

"I'm leaving Saturday."

Literally, as I walked in my house, right after parking my car and turning my key to unlock the door, I was hit with these words. "I'm leaving Saturday." Now, it's one thing to say these words to somebody who isn't expecting to hear them. I'm sure this would have hit them like a ton of bricks. But it's a completely different thing to say these words to someone who's just tired. In fact, sick and tired.

Desperate to hear anything. Tired and praying to just hear something. She…was…me. So, when I heard the words "I'm leaving Saturday," my only response was a question; "Leaving for the weekend or leaving, leaving?" And then…silence.

Silence, followed by "'Leaving, leaving." I'm not sure if I even responded, but I'm sure I'd heard him correctly. I turned around and walked away, but I'd heard him clearly. But this time was different. This time, I'd actually heard the words that I needed to hear.

Not from my husband, but from God. As the words "I'm leaving, leaving" resonated through the canals of my ears and traveled to the epicenter of my comprehension, my place of interpretation, my place of reasoning, and my place of emotion, somehow, they collided with the words being spoken by my loving, heavenly Father.

Almost simultaneously, I heard God say "Enough. You have done enough." It was like a force field was supernaturally placed before my comprehension so those hurtful, spiteful words would be of no effect. I saw his mouth moving and heard exactly what he said. Yet, all I heard and comprehended was "Enough."

You see, this had been a seven-year journey of betrayal, lies, feeble delusion, attempts at reconciliation, the birth of a child that I did not carry in my womb, and so on and so forth. And yet, no divorce. I'd never felt the release for it. I'd never felt it in my spirit. I felt crazy on many days, but I'd never felt the release of divorce.

Somehow, I just knew that I'd know when it was time. God confirmed it one evening while visiting my hairstylist at the time. She told me that I couldn't leave until God released me. Mind you, this woman and I had never ever spoken about what I was feeling in my spirit. In fact, I never talked about the circumstances of marriage with people, so this woman saying these words to me didn't come from her.

They had come through her but were from the mouth of God. And even before I truly understood the significance of my close relationship with God, I had a respect for His voice. Long before He showed me His

face in a dream or long before I fully embraced that I was His eyes and ears on the Earth, I had a respect for His voice. So, as these words rang through my core as confirmation, I stayed.

I endured and kept quiet about a lot of things. Not out of any undying love for my husband, but out of a profound love for God. Somehow, I knew that He'd do a couple of things for me according to His word. He would cover, protect, provide for me, and repay evil for evil. I knew without a shadow of a doubt that He would restore. It wasn't for me to figure out how anything was going to occur.

I just knew it would happen as He (God) said it would. So even when I knew lies were being told, I knew that God would repay. I knew He would provide and restore. Even as a sweet, little boy, oblivious to the mess around him, clueless as to how he'd even entered the world would find himself at my house from time to time, I knew that God would restore. There was no need for useless rhetoric and spiteful words.

There was no need for cussing and yelling. There was no need for checking emails and going through phones. There was no need to do anything but trust God. So, I stayed seven years, until I heard the word "Enough". It wasn't audible, but still and small.

No one shouted it, but I'd heard it loud and clear. I had done what I had been required to do. Within these seven years, we endured a house fire, a car accident, a major injury to the middle boy, a couple of hospital stays for me, a couple of layoffs, a foreclosure, food stamps, unemployment checks, greens, beans, tomatoes, potatoes…you name it, but God. Those knocks hit differently when they come in the form of attacks.

You tend to blame the enemy and rebuke the very thing that God is allowing for a season to refine you, to prune some things and some people away from you, and develop the character that's necessary to carry out the purpose and journey He has for your life. Purpose is messy, disruptive, and embarrassing. Purpose is also confusing, frightening, dark, muddy, and dirty, but purpose is necessary.

It wasn't my past that the enemy was after, it was my purpose. It was my voice. If he could have kept me paralyzed and stuck in the words my husband had spoken over me, I never would have developed the voice to empower those who have been through painful situations. Listen, if you're in a hurtful situation, don't stay there. It will be days when you feel like you can't move forward but move anyway. Move past the betrayal, the lies, and the deceit.

If I can get past what I endured, you can. There is so much power once you decide to endure and move.

Nicole Jones, is the founder of "JNi-coleSpeaks!" which was created to inspire and empower women to create success in every area of their lives. She is a God-focused, Christ-centered influencer, author, business owner, empowerment coach, mother, daughter, sister, and friend.

Nicole is a lover of all people and truly tries to spread the true heart of Christ by being all things to all people. You may not find her in church every Sunday, but what you will find is a heart for people and a heart for God. Nicole is a wonderful sister friend, "Purpose Doula," and Life Strategist.

She is committed to helping women discover their true purpose and live their best lives fully in the abundance that God has to give. She encourages others to use their circumstances, disappointments, and setbacks to create intimate relationships with God without the precepts of religion.

7

Prey to Devour

According to 1 Peter 5:8 (TPT), *our enemy, the devil, roams around incessantly, like a roaring lion looking for its prey to devour.* Strong's Number G2666 states that "*devour*" means to "swallow up or destroy." There was a time in my life when what I did continually to cope, almost destroyed me. During that time, I found that the real enemy was in my mind. Embedded in my subconscious were seeds that prevented me from moving forward in life.

I would get so far only to come to a stretching halt. I could not explain what was going on, but the circling led me to bouts of depression and an inability to progress. Every time I found myself in that place, I isolated myself from everything and everyone. I may have been physically present but mentally and emotionally I was not there. I was unable to share what was on my heart with anyone without dismissiveness.

I was dismissed with scripture, being told to "pray about it" or "just be grateful." I knew something was wrong. I knew there was a deeper work to be done, but I had no idea where to turn. After the flood of

2016, I isolated myself for the last time. Although I maintained during this traumatic event, I got back into my home and the walls started closing in on me. I had not grieved that loss.

I saved face by being the strong woman I was expected to be because talking about how I was feeling meant I was being "ungrateful." The relationship I was in only brought out the worst in me and I was experiencing sabotage and psychological abuse from those in an organization who had mastered the use of smoke screens and shape shifting. Once again, I was at such a broken state; a pluck would have been the end.

This last time I learned that each time I isolated myself it was harder to pull through. This is it, I thought. There is no way I will make it out this time. It was dark, grimy, cold, and lonely. Internally I was screaming for help, but my screams went unnoticed. I could not focus, I could not pray, I could not move. I felt like I was trapped in another body. My thoughts and dreams tormented me.

Every waking hour was depressing. My tears were hidden by the shower as I sat at its base screaming to break free. There were times I would pump gas and thoughts plagued my mind to drink it, purging the world of such a failure. In those times of isolation, I became prey to the devourer.

I had broken community. I had given up and I allowed what was before me to shape the outcome. My fight was gone. This was by far the worst out of all the times I had resorted to isolation. Isolating is very dangerous. Every traumatic experience flooded me and almost consumed me.

I recounted the abuse, self-destructive behavior, disappointments, hurt, shame, and feeling like I was all alone. I was misunderstood, had my character assassinated, lied on, being called a devil, and even had a loved one threaten to kill me. And no one ever had my back. I thought of the times I almost died. It all came back to collect.

I sat night after night holding all of that, like on the edge of a cliff. The real enemy, the subconscious mind, almost devoured me. There was no man in a red suit with horns. My enemy was the unprocessed pain, my enemy was the trauma that had not been overcome. Those things that laid dormant in my subconscious mind all erected at once. I was in a greater battle than ever.

Wounds love isolation. Dark places are cesspools for depression and suicidal ideation. I was in such a sunken place at that time that I thought there was no way I would come out. There wasn't a rope long enough to be thrown down to pull me out. Each time I tried to come not having released the pain, I fell back farther.

I could not get a good grip; it was all too heavy. I was fatigued and my hands were sore from the repeated attempts to break free. My body was bruised from the stones thrown that pushed me back deeper. Death was an escape that I felt I needed because there was no way out.

Then the day came. I saw a light shining down in the pit and a voice that said, "Just let your heart break." That was the beginning of my journey to wholeness. I laid in that sunken place and I allowed myself to feel what I avoided for years. My tears created a puddle beneath me but this time I was not drowning. This time I was healing.

I read a book entitled "*The Bait of Satan*" by John Bevere, that liberated me even more. It did not happen all at once. There was a process. I still hurt, but I could speak. I cried daily, but I could rest knowing each tear was being bottled. Every day I had to continuously work at my freedom. I would not die but live is what I quoted from the Bible each day.

I started seeing a therapist who immediately pointed out the little girl in me needed healing. I resumed coaching from a phenomenal teacher I met via social media and by then I had connected with another coach who walked me through soul detoxing. I got my life back, my purpose was made manifest, I was given tools to help others and day by day restoration came.

I was in pursuit of a whole me and nothing or no one would get in my way. Anything that was not conducive to healing I walked away free and unapologetically.

LaToya Nicole, is a passionate coach, consultant, and business owner with a zest for success. She is the owner of "S.O.LO. Coaching & Consulting LLC," where she operates as a Certified Life Coach and Journal Therapist, author, and virtual organizer. As a success enthusiast, LaToya prides herself on maintaining mental health and living life purposefully, aligned continuously to her vision, and healing organizationally.

She has suffered from childhood trauma and has made it her life's work to help others heal and evolve into the people they were pre-trauma. As a newly enrolled student at the Therapon Institute for Certified Belief Therapy, LaToya believes that she has the lifetime opportunity to transform the lives of people faced with similar challenges. She is a hard worker, a keen visionary, and a natural leader with a servant's heart. She has found this path to be abundantly rewarding.

8

Defying the Invisible Evil

Defying the invisible forces that chase us in life is fundamental for survival. In the life of teenage girls, these forces may take different shapes. My story is about overcoming an eating disorder in a country that had barely heard about the condition, as a teenager, with limited resources, but a will to live and achieve the greater things in life, which I managed to accomplish.

I grew up in what would be considered a one-bedroom apartment in Eastern Europe, a formerly communist country. My bed was in the kitchenette, and since I dreamt about having my own room for virtually my whole teenage life. I adorned two kitchen cupboards' insides with pictures and drawings that I would normally put on the walls of my own room, that is if I had one.

It was a rather normal childhood, as normal as it could be when we are referring to the child of divorced parents. I withdrew in my own version of the world, and just grabbed what I had in my power with dear life. I was an ambitious child and growing up in a third world country did not necessarily align with my vision for my future. The problem was that I had this body between me and my brilliant future that I was watching about on TV.

We had MTV, and other fancy foreign channels showing these pretty thin girls that looked so happy and careless. I remember writing in my diary somewhere that when I am older, I would have a boyfriend and will wear makeup and cute clothes. My country did not sell cute clothes for overweight middle schoolers. So, my mom had to redo adult clothing to fit me and it looked rather funny.

I was miserable with my weight, and dreamt about being thin, as that was the image I built in my head from the media and other sources. My mom took me to a doctor who recommended a diet, so I tried that and failed. I tried again and again at no avail. When I was about fifteen, I decided I was fed up with everything.

All my other classmates by then had boyfriends and here I was, miserable because of my weight, and simply feeling stuck in my own body, crashed under the happy face of thin and pretty women that the media had helped to instill in my head. I tried dieting again, but this time seriously. I gradually decreased the amount of food I was eating daily and just kept busy to keep from thinking about food. Well, I succeeded.

When I was at my ideal weight for my height, everyone in my family (who is generally overweight), was so happy for me, congratulating me, and appearing happy for me. I even met a boy who became my first boyfriend, and I was simply at the top of the world. Everything appeared so

normal at this point, and I was simmering in giddiness from the new wardrobe I was getting with all the cute clothes.

I had already dreamt about the makeup I was starting to wear, and everything in between. It was a rather masked happiness. Meanwhile, I was throwing my dear and sweet grandma who used to love to feed me beyond satiety into a panic attack because when I went to visit her I only ate a single tomato for the whole day and nothing else. I had gradually shrunk my intake portions to almost nothing.

So instead of maintaining my ideal weight, I kept on losing the pounds and eventually I also lost my period for about eight months. My mom had to ask me whether I was pregnant, and of course, that was not a possibility, but I know she was worried nonetheless. At that time, I even wrote to the National Association of Eating Disorders to get some insights with what was going on with me.

I was literally clueless about eating disorders and even though now I know that is what I had at that time, nobody around me even suspected or had heard of it, so they had no idea that I needed help. Well, I did need help big time, as it turned out, and my mom truly got worried when one night I passed out in the hallway on the way from the bathroom.

She was very stern and made me eat some more fruits and started talking about going to the private clinic (healthcare in third world countries is not entirely reliable unless it is a private office, which could still be questionable). I took the little savings I had and went to pay for some expensive hormonal blood testing to determine why I did not have a period for so long.

Upon the visit with the physician, he told me that if I had waited a little longer without a period, I would possibly have lost the ability to bear my own kids. That was my wake-up call. I always wanted to have kids, four, to be precise. So, I shook off the dieting, started on hormonal and vitamin shots, and began to eat a little more every day until I got to the normal portion. I gained some of the weight back, but most importantly, I had gotten my period back as well.

Today, some almost twenty years after that time, I am looking back and cannot help but shake my head sadly, that I did not have the resources to support me and the knowledge to understand what I was going through. Yet, in spite of it all, I succeeded in going through an eating disorder almost by myself at the tender age of sixteen and avoided being infertile for life, because of the thin happy woman image that the media had put in my mind.

I did end up having the four babies I always dreamt of, and now having lived in America for almost seventeen years, know-how teenage girls continue looking up to the media for the perfect image, completely unaware of how easy it is to miss a problem until it is too late. That is why I try to help other girls and mothers nowadays and educate them on how important it is to be there and be knowledgeable and resourceful for our daughters.

Zlatka Rankine, a budding author-to-be, has been writing since she was youngin' in the fiction genre, and recently tried out non-fiction for fun. With a rich background in business, healthcare, and hospitality, she is an expert on many academic and business topics that make her a versatile resource.

Her experience is further augmented by her expertise with her crew, her four children that she adores and encourages to do their best and beyond. Being a bi-lingual fanatic reader since her middle school years made Zlatka develop a good eye for writing and helped her in her craft throughout the years. Her hobbies, beyond immersing in the local libraries, include swimming, cooking, movies, and having fun with the crew.

Follow Zlatka "Zee" Rankine on IG: zranks2020

9

A Life with No Purpose

There I was, just lying there in my bed with tears running down my face wondering, "What purpose do I serve? Am I really fit to live?" At the time, I was twenty-four years old and was the manager at a fast food chain. I absolutely hated that job, but I was good at it and I made decent money. I felt out of place because I desired more! I wanted my life to serve a purpose.

I kept thinking that I had no purpose. My mind was filled with those thoughts. The enemy had me thinking that because I hadn't figured it out yet that I wasn't meant to live. Day after day I would lie in the bed and fantasize about a more fulfilling life. A life that I loved, a life where I was successful, and could live out my dreams.

But what was my dream? I was lost. I had no idea what I wanted to be. I only knew that I wanted to make a major impact on people's life and lead by example. I wanted to be a woman that my sons admired. I wanted to be a woman that my husband could brag about.

However, I was only a woman who had a job that she hated. I had no faith in myself. I couldn't see past the moment or the season I was in. I felt like my life would never change. I felt like I would be unhappy forever.

How could a beautiful woman feel so empty inside?

How could I think that I was worthless?

How could I think that my life didn't have purpose?

My husband would constantly ask me what I wanted to do and I would get very frustrated because I didn't have a clue. He had figured it out and here I was lost and didn't know what to do. This went on for years, then I finally decided that it was time for a change.

I decided that I would think highly of myself. I decided I would dress the part. I decided that I would step out on faith and go for whatever it was that I was searching for. However, I still didn't know what that was. He kept asking me what I was passionate about and I did not know.

I've always worked very hard at whatever it was that I put my hands to do. I never really wanted to attend a four-year university. I thought that this was a generational thing. My mom didn't attend college so why should I? But I saw everyone else around me graduating from college.

Deep down inside I despised those who I thought had it together. How could God bless them with purpose and forget about me? This is not what I dreamed of as a child. The saying when you change the way you think you change your life is very true. I started thinking differently and my life changed.

I started seeing myself as the person I wanted to become and not the person I was. Life started turning around. I had finally got a job that I loved. One day my husband came home with an idea. He had written down a few business names and told me to choose one. One of the names he had written was "A Sweet Treat," which was the name of my Instagram page.

He had come up with the idea to start a mobile snowball stand. In my time of need he didn't look down on me, he helped me. The next morning, I went to the bank to inquire about a loan. While I was waiting for approval, we started to look for a stand. We found the perfect truck. The bank called and said, "You are approved."

This was the beginning of something great but also the end of a dark place. My husband had helped me find my confidence. He helped me find my purpose. We started "A Sweet Treat" in March 2014. Our first business together. It's a small business but it's ours. "A Sweet Treat" gave me my confidence back. I now know that God's timing is perfect.

I can't count the times He has come through at the right time. That time really changed my life. What I went through was meant to break me and to destroy my marriage. If the enemy can have your mind, he can have your life. He comes to steal, kill, and destroy. So, he will steal your dreams, he will kill your spirit, and ultimately destroy you; if that's what you allow him to do.

I'm still here for a reason. My life has meaning, and I want to encourage you. Your life serves purpose. God can use anything in your life for your purpose. In spite of the enemy trying to break me, I am a strong woman who now uplifts other women. I now encourage people from day to day. Even if it's just telling them that they are beautiful. I am a better mother because now I know who I am. I am strong, confident, and phenomenal.

In spite of the enemy trying to break me, I am stronger than I've ever been. I now teach financial classes. I help women start small businesses. I'm a mentor in the community and I lead praise. My advice to you if you are struggling to find your purpose, it's okay.

God has perfect timing and He will reveal your purpose to you in due time. It may be a situation that reveals your purpose. Your thoughts will take control of you if you let them. I encourage you to write down your affirmations every day and climb out of that dark place that you are in. Nothing comes from fear and procrastination.

Go for it!!! You will never know what you are good at if you don't try. Keep going no matter how hard it gets.

Tanika Kendrick, is the Owner/Operator of "A Sweet Treat Snowballs." She has a background in management. Tanika is a first-time author who aspires to do more projects in the future. She has been educating her community on financial literacy for the past three years. She is the mother of three, who enjoys uplifting women and leading praise and worship at her church.

Tanika and her family enjoy vlogging on YouTube. You can catch them on "The Kendrick Family Channel."

Tanika can be reached on Facebook as- Tanika Kendrick.
Email- tanikabuchanank@gmail.com

10

Delayed but Not Denied

As a child I dreamt of marrying a great man and having three kids, but no one ever taught me how to do this. I was, however, taught to work hard and be rock solid at my career, and that's what I did. I just assumed the husband and children would naturally follow. Let me tell you how wrong I was.

I spent my twenties and thirties having a blast. I was climbing the corporate ladder, traveling the world with my girlfriends, and buying and selling real estate. I was getting it. I was also dating frequently but rarely getting beyond anything casual. I remember one year in my twenties where I had seventeen first dates and no seconds, lol.

I was bypassing men for every reason imaginable. You've heard the excuses, "He's too nice, he can't dress, he doesn't excite me, he doesn't have a passport." Yes, I said them all. You see I had time (or so I thought) so I wasn't settling for anybody. Lol I was a complete mess.

Fast forward to my fortieth birthday. I spent a weekend in NYC and came back to a huge birthday dinner with family and friends. I had also just gotten promoted to Director at my job, but something was missing. What happened to that childhood dream of the husband and three kids? How did I get here?

This was not supposed to be my life. That night I prayed to God saying "Hey, don't get me wrong, I love these blessings you've given me, but I think you forgot something. So if you could just rectify that, I'll be grateful, Amen."

And then weeks, months, and years passed by and no husband, no kids, despite my very best efforts. See I figured if I just put all of the energy I had put into my career into my personal life I could knock this thing out in no time. Silly me, oh how I know God laughed. But hey I'm a "Type A" girl so if option one doesn't work out, let's move to option two.

I may not be able to get a husband but there are other ways to become a mom. And no, before you go there, I was not about to trap one of my dates into unsuspecting parenthood. I decided to adopt (please note the use of the word I). I got my parents on board and started my research. I met with an adoption consultant and an agency.

I was going full steam ahead until one night, while lying in my bed, I heard God just as clearly as if He were sitting next to me. He said, "Are you Sarah? Why are you trying to do for yourself what only I can do for you?" (If you're not familiar with Sarah's story read Genesis 16).

I had never received a clearer message. All efforts toward adoption stopped. I got that part right – but I assumed the message meant that God was sending me the husband and I would birth my baby the "traditional" way. So once again I began looking for "Mr. Right" to cross my path, excited about what was in store.

Do you know that every man I met after that was incapable of having a child either by illness or vasectomy? I felt like I was in a comedy skit and the joke was on me. This time I was all out of options. So I did the only thing I knew how to do. I sat before God and I cried, prayed, screamed, and ultimately humbled myself.

I said "I'm done Lord. I surrender this desire to you." I remember saying "If this isn't your will for me, I trust you to still give me an abundant life," for the word says, "You will have life and have it abundantly." I must admit I didn't really believe those words when I started praying them. I couldn't see my life without being a mom. But I kept praying that prayer.

You see, sometimes you have to speak it until you see it. I didn't stop praying for my desire to marry and mother, but I knew that God would fulfill me even if it didn't happen. Then one day a single friend announced on social media that she had adopted a son, and my heart leaped. I went before the Lord that day with my desire to adopt and asked for his blessing and confirmation if this was his will.

Notice this time I did it differently. I sought God first. On the day before my forty-fifth birthday I was having lunch with my mom. She told me that being a mother was the greatest gift she had ever received, and she prayed that one day I would know that joy. The very next day, I signed the contract with the agency and eighteen months later my daughter was born. That was two years ago, and it has been the best two years of my life.

As I look back on the moment when God stopped me from moving forward with the adoption process, I realize there were two things at play. One, He needed my heart to change. I had made my desire for marriage and motherhood my God and only He could hold that place. And two, God was preparing me to mother a specific child and she was going to be born at a specific time. The wait, you see, was purposeful.

I don't know what you are believing God for or what part of your journey has taken an unexpected turn, but here are the lessons I learned along the way. Every path is unique. If you let go of your preconceived notion of what it's supposed to look like, and trust God to give you what you need, the destination will be greater than you ever could have imagined. Now let me go have a talk with God about that husband, wink.

Nicole Long, is the owner of "Twinkle Toes Nanny Agency West Cobb." She started her life in entrepreneurship after becoming a mom through the gift of adoption. Prior to Twinkle Toes, Nicole had a successful finance career in corporate America spanning twenty years. One of the highlights of Nicole's career was facilitating finance training, for Coca-Cola associates in Lagos, Nigera and Nairobi, Kenya.

She holds a Bachelor's Degree in Accounting and an MBA with a concentration in Finance, both from the School of Business and Industry at Florida A&M University. Nicole has an intense focus on community service and is active on several boards. She has also served as a facilitator for learning and development for organizations such as Coca-Cola, AICPA, Inroads, NABA, Jack and Jill, Monica Motivates, NBMBAA, UW of Greater Atlanta, and Deloitte.

Nicole's proudest accomplishment is being mom to two-year-old Madison. Contact Nicole at nicole@twinkletoesnanny.com.

11

The Unidentified Little Girl

I think I can speak for millions of women when I say that many fathers broke their daughter's heart long before any other man came along into her life and that first heartbreak cuts the deepest. I have very vague memories of my father as a little girl. My mother told me stories of the physical abuse that she endured while married to him as a young woman in her twenties.

I was blessed to never have seen it myself or to not remember it. She told me one particular story that stuck in my mind about the time my father shot himself in the chest to scare her into taking him back. You know, it's funny that as a little girl no matter what I heard about my dad I just wanted to have my own relationship with him. I needed to know that he wanted me as a daughter, I needed to hear that he was proud to be my dad.

I wanted to feel protected and cherished as most little girls do. I was about six years old when my parents finally divorced for good and my contact with him became close to non-existent. I remember several occasions when he would tell my mother to have me ready so he could come pick me up to spend the day with him. I waited for hours and he never showed up.

Every time he would get my hopes up, I truly believed that he was coming this time. I just knew my dad wasn't going to let me down again, but I was wrong. The hopeful and optimistic little girl was replaced by the hurt and angry little girl who made herself a promise that she would never let her father break her heart again.

It was weird to me that all of the years of my childhood my father knew where I was, and I knew where he was, but we never had a relationship. He just stopped reaching out and my fear of rejection wouldn't allow me to contact him either. I became fiercely independent at a very young age, promising myself that I didn't need a father and I was probably better off without one.

I vowed to always count on myself and nobody else. I didn't understand that the little heartbroken girl was still very much alive inside of me. She was hiding behind the mask of independence. That lack of validation from my father affected my choices in men and led me to have a series of unhealthy and toxic relationships.

It seemed that the more dysfunctional they were the more we were attracted to each other. It's crazy how our suppressed demons will be drawn to the hidden demons of another person. My messed up thinking made me believe that I could fix them and also prove that I was worthy of being loved, cherished and protected. I didn't have my own identity. I was always searching for self-worth and validation from a man.

This path just led me deeper into feelings of worthlessness because I continued to get involved with men who were just as damaged as I was. The saying that "you attract what you put out," aren't just empty words, it's very true. It took me going through two failed marriages to really take a step back and let God enter into places in my mind and heart that I had never let Him enter before.

Once I really let Him work on me and show me the ugly, broken parts of me that I never acknowledged, that's when I found my worth. I had been looking for my worth in my earthly father and he couldn't give it to me. I looked for my worth in relationships with men to fill the void that my earthly father left, I never found it.

When I turned back to the Heavenly Father who created me in His image and loves me unconditionally, that's when I began to understand the greatness and the beauty that I possess. I am fearfully and wonderfully made. I love my strengths and I respect my weaknesses. We talk a lot about self-love these days. I believe that you can't have true self love if you don't let God show you who you really are and fall in love with what you see.

The next phase of my healing was to truly forgive my father. I want you to understand that sometimes in life you will have to accept the apology that you never received. I let go of the anger and the blame that I placed on my father's absence in my life. What if he had stayed in my life? Would I be the woman I am today?

I believe that this experience was chosen for me. It made me aware, it made me compassionate, it made me become the voice for women just like me who aren't able to verbalize their experience. Life's lessons and the wisdom of God has revealed to me that my father had his own story and I don't know why he couldn't be a father to me.

Just because a person has the physical ability to create a child doesn't mean they were called by God to be a parent. I have made peace with the fact that he just didn't know how, and he may have never seen an example to follow. As I close this chapter, I want to acknowledge that my father died six days ago, and I didn't know how to feel about the news.

It felt like getting the news of a stranger's death but as time passed, I really began to grieve his loss because I never asked him why and now, I will never know. In spite of it all, the little girl in me and the woman I have become can agree that we love our earthly father and our Heavenly Father.

Rest in peace Ray Daniel Warren

Erica Warren, is a Best-Selling author of "Dear Young Woman." She is a passionate cheerleader for women who want to speak their truth and heal from their past. Her motto is "I will be the person that I needed when I was younger." Erica is a former customer service agent in the banking industry who is now an independent agent in the financial services industry.

She loves to educate the next generation about money and how to leave a legacy behind for their families. Erica was born and raised in Franklinton, LA and is now a current resident of Hammond, LA. She is a proud mother of four sons ranging in ages from twenty-three to thirteen.

To learn more about this author you can follow her on Instagram @e_class100, on Facebook @Author Erica Warren or you can catch an episode of her podcast called, "The Code Of Sisterhood" on Spotify, Google podcasts or Anchor.fm.

12

A Motherless Child

I was twelve years old when my mother died from AIDS. She contracted HIV from her boyfriend who inserted needles into his arms, beat her, and had his way with her once the high kicked in. Her death was sudden. She had many doctor and hospital visits during the last few months of her life. We never questioned any of the visits.

She hid the disease from my siblings and I. It wasn't until two weeks before she died in 1991 that I asked the question to a family member, "Does my mother have AIDS?" Not only did my mother die, but I had no relationship with my father. Being a parentless child, I was just navigating through life without any supervision and guidance. Throughout the years I buried these feelings so deep that I was just floating through life with a lot of emotional trauma.

In many instances in my life I felt like I was dying while living. This caused me to make many poor decisions, never fully trusting individuals, having a closed heart, and constantly feeling like I did not belong. As a motherless child, I moved around a lot from the ages of twelve to nineteen years old, living with different family members in different states. Each time I could almost smell when it was my time to move along as if I overstayed my welcome.

I was almost homeless twice and by the grace of God, my temporary illegal stay at the college dormitory provided a roof over my head and the stability of a home. Moving so often forced me to keep an eye on every dollar that I earned trying to survive but, in the end, it taught me how to manage my money and financial literacy. One of the poor decisions that I made was dating drug dealers at a very young age.

I was a product of my environment. This was my norm. At the time, dating a drug dealer meant loyalty, fast money, and unconditional love that I was missing from my mother. It was one of my methods of survival. But as I entered college and was exposed to different walks of life, I realized dating and being exposed to the drug game was hell living on earth. My conscience began to bother me, and I could no longer participate in a world that killed my mother.

As an adult and in college, I hid the passing of my mother from many people around me. I was ashamed, lost, angry, and most of all confused. I buried the feelings of loneliness, depression, and missing the unconditional love of my mother. I struggled my entire life trying to understand how and why this was my walk in life. It wasn't until I became a mother myself that I understood the depth of my grief that never really went away.

Once I started to fully accept and embrace the passing of my mother, I slowly began to heal. I began to work on myself both emotionally and spiritually. The progression took years of consistent work and relentless persistence. As a part of my healing process I started practicing yoga. At the beginning of every class the instructors ask you to state your intentions. Setting an intention means choosing something that you want to amplify or cultivate.

I choose to cultivate internal peace and calmness. Yoga has allowed me to unlearn and release the years of anger, grief, and disturbance that existed in my spirit because of the absence of my mother. I now look at life's storms as passing clouds and yoga has taught me to remain calm during the storms. It has also taught me to breathe, let it go, and to forgive. I've learned that when we don't forgive, we are causing internal suffering.

It is like a bad sore that never heals and keeps agitating our soul. I choose to forgive my mother for not being here to guide me through life, for not being here to be the grandmother to my children, and for not patting me on the back when I needed it the most. I have also forgiven myself for holding on to the anger, grief, and confusion.

Forgiveness is self-love and a gift you give to yourself in the middle of confusion. It is a constant reminder to be compassionate and kind to yourself. Your circumstances does not determine where you go in life. Your circumstances have redirected your life. When we accept that we are not in control of our walk in life, we alleviate depression, fear, and anxiety. I would encourage anyone who is a motherless child or has lost a parent to believe in redirection.

My life has been redirected numerous times and it started with the death of my mother. For example, I moved to a new state after my mother passed away and as a result my environment changed. I was now living amongst and was exposed to middle and upper-class families. As a result of this exposure, the conversations were different, and the conversation at the time was, "What University are you going to?"

I applied to colleges and universities and ended up going to college on a full scholarship. When redirection occurs, it is an end to a new beginning. It is the stepping-stone to what God has in store for you. No matter how hard life is and you feel like breaking down you are actually breaking free. As a motherless child, I learned early on how to survive in a cold world and how to change the trajectory and generational pathology of my son's future.

I now realize that all of my life experiences are a part of my gift. My story is a blessing and a living testament to help others. Release the anger, stress, and frustration that is blocking you from existing in a peaceful and calm space. Right now, at this very moment let it go and breathe. I encourage everyone reading this to give yourself permission to be happy, centered, and love yourself unconditionally.

Candice Morales, is the Founder/CEO of "Budget for Me LLC." She is a graduate of Long Island University in Brooklyn, New York, and holds a Bachelor of Science Degree in Finance. Candice learned at a very young age the importance of financial literacy.

She faced many challenges as a young adult forcing her to keep a close eye on every dollar she earned to survive. The life skills she acquired ultimately helped her later in life and is now passionate about helping other gain control of their finances and make informed financial decisions.

Candice is a successful small business owner, and mother of two. She is on a mission to educate and inspire others about financial freedom and discuss why their current circumstances does not determine where they go in life, but instead redirects it.

www.thebudgetforme.com
Email: thebudgetforme@gmail.com
Book Purchase: www.payhip.com/candicemorales
IG: GlaMorales

13

More Than a Conqueror

What started out as a typical fun summer day took a horrific turn. I must have been about eight years old. We, my brother, my dad, and myself were outside and my stepfather challenged us. He had us run around the house and whoever quit first would be the loser, so we started running. After about two times, my brother quit and of course that made me the winner, right?

So, I thought. He told me to keep running because I was fat and needed to lose weight. So, I kept running thinking, my brother is fat too, so why did he get to stop? I told him I needed to go to the bathroom, but he said I was just trying to get out of running and I had to keep going until he said stop. Well, ended up wetting my clothes. I hated myself so much for that.

I was so humiliated. I loved my daddy, but that day I began to hate him. Fast forward about four years and I was about twelve years old. On the school bus, one of the kids said to me, "My momma said she saw your daddy in town yesterday," and I said, "No she didn't, my daddy was at work yesterday." She said, "I'm not talking about Wayne, he is not your daddy, your daddy is Ray Warren."

I said, "You don't know what you are talking about." I couldn't wait to get home to ask my mom. I just knew she was going to say that it was all wrong. I got home, went to her room and repeated what was told to me and the expression on her face gave me the answer. She looked as if she had seen a ghost and my heart sank.

She told me that the kid was right. I asked her why she never told me. She said she was waiting for the right time. I sat there dumbfounded and in disbelief. I then knew why I could not stop running around the house that day. That day changed my life.

The fact that I was bullied by my stepfather, abandoned by my biological father, and lied to and betrayed by my mother, pummeled me into a life of drinking, promiscuity, clubbing, stealing, and even landing myself in jail. Fast forward about seven years to March 31, 1993; I made a phone call that would change my life forever. I made a phone call to someone that showed interest in me to come pick me up from college.

We ended up at some apartments and one thing led to another. After it was over, I told him that I was pregnant. He called me stupid and took me back to the dorm. I got home that Friday, told my mom that I was pregnant. She told me I was lying. I didn't say it again. She figured it out after a few months. I called him a month later and told him I needed to see him.

He picked me up and I told him I really was pregnant. He said he didn't want any more kids, and told me, "To get rid of it." I told him I wasn't going to. His eyes glazed over, and he pulled out an ivory handled pistol, put it to my head and said, "I will kill you if you don't." Well, me being me I said, "You might as well pull the trigger, because I am not going to kill my baby."

Then I prayed and said, "God, if you get me out of this, I will not put myself in this situation again." He came to himself, put the gun away, and took me back to the dorm. That night set me on course to becoming the woman of God that I am today. My path up until then was dark. I realized that I wasn't just living for myself anymore. I had to change. It wasn't easy.

There were steps that I had to take, and I want to share some of those steps with you today. I had to take an inventory of my life and remove all the negatives. I developed a prayer life, and that was my saving grace. It was time for me to develop a relationship with God. It was a daily process, but I was determined. I had to change my surroundings.

I graduated from college that May and was set to begin at Alcorn State University that coming August. I made the decision to set out, and work on me. I came home, got a job, and spent time with God. I began to learn how to love me and know that God was the only Father that I needed. Was it tough, yes, but I kept pushing forward.

I was becoming more than a conqueror. The enemy wanted me to kill myself, yes suicide knocked on my door, but I did not answer. I have an overwhelming victory because of Jesus. I can remember crying out to God and asking, "Why me God? Why did I have to go through what I went through as a child, why me? Why am I going through this right now?"

I felt ashamed, I was in despair, and at my lowest point. But the more I pursued God, reading His word, praying, and spending time with likeminded people, I started seeing myself rise out of the ashes. And I was not going back. I had a driving force; I had that baby growing in my womb and I knew that I had to make a better life for her. And I did.

I've been down and in despair, but no more. I am more than a conqueror. I didn't just survive, I thrived. I am not just existing I am living, because of my faith in God and His unwavering love for me. I am more than a conqueror, through Christ.

Ketrice Keys, is a serial entrepreneur, motivational speaker, licensed evangelist, speaker development coach, and life coach. She is the wife of Curtis Keys, a mother of three beautiful children, and grandmother of twin boys. She is currently employed by Mississippi State Department of Health as a registered nurse. Ketrice has been in the nursing profession for the past twenty years.

She is the founder of "Ketrice Keys Enterprises," and is adamant about equipping women with the keys to turn off the power of the enemy in their lives and activate the power of God. She is committed to inspiring women to uncover their purpose and pursue their passions. She believes that we all have a story that does not belong to us, but to the world. Ketrice empowers women to share their stories, thereby freeing themselves and others as well.

Email: ketricekeys@gmail.com
Facebook: https://www.facebook.com/ketricekeys.keys

14

A Soul Thirsty for Love

At the tender age of seven, my soul was tapered with a sexual demon I was not aware of. Shaking in fear, I become a prisoner by fear and silence. When I was ten, that same demon visited me once again and this time took my innocence without my permission. Here I am at a very young age, lost and drifting through the wind.

I had this huge void in my body that needed filling but did not know how to fill it. I was hurt, angry, ashamed, and the pain led me to the dark side. Turning fifteen was when I thought I had a boyfriend who I could trust and who I thought loved me for me. Sooner than later, I was about to find out his true intentions.

April 7th, 2009 my "boyfriend" and I were texting back and forth about being intimate and yes of course I was nervous about it, but I trusted him and gave in. When the time came to go forth and fulfill the action I hesitated and told him "No I want to wait and just talk." He blew my mind when he told me "Relax this isn't your first time you are easy anyway." That very moment is when my soul became officially numb to any and everything.

I laid there for those few moments of the action, got up and went on with my day like nothing ever happened. I pretended to be happy and okay with what just happened but deep inside, once again, I became a prisoner of silence. Not having a father in my life at a young age made me wonder and search for the love of a father a young girl would be craving for. I went on with my life and tried to pick up the pieces and do better for myself.

I attended college finally on the right road to a new start but I was still a prisoner of silence in my mind and not breaking free of that led me to another world I was not expecting to live for the next four years. In college, I was hanging with my buddies very frequently. I started to club more and study less. I began to skip class because my hangover was so bad, I couldn't focus in class. College life was exciting for me because I did not experience fun with friends in my teenage years.

I tried marijuana for the first time while I was living in college and then one night while hanging out with some people, I tried cocaine. The rush and adrenaline I felt was amazing. It made me feel like my soul was alive once again. My first high made me want to do it again every time I used. I wanted to feel alive, worthy, and loved. Of course, I eventually dropped out of college and returned home to my parents.

Here I am back home and not around the excited life I was once living. I began to search for the drug and came across another guy who I thought loved me but was only using me and enabling my bad habits. This boyfriend was a drug dealer which made it very easy for me to get my fix without my parents noticing what I was doing. The drug using secret was kept hidden for a while and I knew I was not going to get caught because I was a functioning addict.

My boyfriend at the time ended up going to jail which led me to finding another addiction since I did not have my enabler anymore. I turned twenty-one shortly after and began drinking heavily because I was finally legal and could get all the liquor I wanted to drink. For two years, I was drinking liquor like a fish and was doing all kinds of risky things.

Due to my soul being so thirsty, I tried to quench its thirst by drinking, cutting on myself, attempting suicide and using pills until I became pregnant at the age of twenty-three with twin boys. When the doctor told me I was expecting twins I began to panic because I knew I had to stop using drugs and alcohol for the sake of my precious babies.

The moment I realized I had to finally face my demons from childhood is when I allowed Jesus Christ to enter my life and take control of my mind. I got on my knees and wept for hours talking to God and asking him to remove the taste of drugs and alcohol out my mouth and come into my heart to fill my huge void I had for so many years. God did just that and once I fully trusted Him, I could finally see the light and know what true love really was.

I ended up having my twins at twenty-five weeks. They were one pound each. Even though they were tiny, they fought like David did in the Bible and conquered the giant. Within those three months in the hospital, I learned very quickly I would not survive this journey mentally without God, my mom, and family support.

My twins were discharged in December of 2017. Being a single mom was not the plan, but I enjoyed every minute of it and continued to let God take lead of my life. Everything is about timing. While I was focused on motherhood, I reconnected with a friend I had known for five years. He welcomed my children and I with open arms and has not let us go since.

I told God very specifically what I wanted my husband to be and He gave me just that. I overcame my demons once I realized who was in control-God. I would not do anything different in my past because I would not be living this wonderful life I have in the present. Keeping God first in everything is what keeps me striving for greatness.

Najadanika Simmons, is a mother of NICU twin boys who are two years of age now. She is currently a student at Southwest Mississippi Community College studying to be a social worker. Naja loves to attend church faithfully, help out within her family, and most of all she loves being a mother.

In Naja's free time, she often writes poetry about love, God, and nature. She has a heart of gold and a bubbly personality. She has a hard exterior and a soft interior which by the way, is that of a hopeless romantic.

Najadanika Simmons can be reached on Facebook, Instagram and by email (snaja12@yahoo.com).

15

Girl Get Up, and Remember Who You Are

In October 2005, after having to start over post Hurricane Katrina, I moved to Memphis, TN with my two-and-a-half-year-old son and fiancé with hopes of having a better life. Shortly after arriving I discovered I was expecting. A surge of emotions had taken over my mind, body and soul. I was excited because I love children, and I loved being a mother. I was also scared because I was moving to a new city with unfamiliar faces.

It was a lot, yet I was up for the adventure. Upon arriving to Memphis, it all started out to be as good as could be, considering all that had transpired. Here I was, months shy of my twentieth birthday. I was a mother, a new mother to be, I had become a wife, and I was in a new city with new possibilities. This was it! Starting over didn't seem so bad.

WRONG! Let's fast forward to December 2005. I went to my obstetrics appointment as I had previously done, but this visit was different. We completed the ultrasound as normal. All looked OK, not great but OK. I found out my baby girl was in distress. She was experiencing issues with her heart rate, but the physician was comfortable enough to send me home.

So, I did just that- I went home and cried. I'll be honest, I didn't pray. I just cried because I knew something was wrong. Well I returned the next week to the dr expecting to hear some news, but nothing had prepared me for the news I was about to hear. BOOM! The physician uttered the words, "Teara, your unborn daughter has Polysplenia Syndrome which will also encompass other developmental abnormalities. If she survives, she will be disabled and unable to live a normal life."

My body went numb, my mind went blank, my soul was shattered. I managed to get off of the table and somehow made it home, placed my key in the door, turned the knob and fell on the floor. How? Why? When? Were amongst the questions swarming around in my head. Later that evening I explained it to my husband all the physician had told me at the appointment earlier.

He didn't say anything, turned the lights out, and went to bed. I was expecting something- shouting, anger, rage, something! I got nothing. Days turned to weeks and it was time to return for another appointment. This turned out to be just as gut wrenching as the last one- we found out she wasn't going to make it… NO WAY. WHAT?! Not me, not my baby. Lord, what did I do? Lord, what did she do? I was angry at myself, my husband, and God. I was mad at the world.

Days turned into weeks and it was appointment time again. I was strangely hoping that they would do another ultrasound and she would be better and in a couple of months, I would be holding my princess in my arms. I returned to the appointment and sat on the table with my legs dangling on the side saying to myself, "Teara she will be fine, Teara she will be fine." This actually turned out to be the worst appointment ever.

The ultrasound was done, and the screen was completely blacked out. She was gone, my sweet baby girl was gone. The world would not be graced by her presence. February 6th 2006, I gave birth to a beautiful three pound baby girl. I was able to dress her in the cutest yellow floral dress that I had ever seen.

I then had to hand her over to the nurses for them to take her away. At that time, post Katrina, because she was stillborn and I didn't know the things I know now, she was buried by the state of Tennessee, in the city of Memphis, in a large public graveyard with a number. My sweet baby girl will be remembered by a number. I felt like the worst parent on the planet.

I wasn't the same after that day and neither was my husband, or our marriage. He began to draw closer to the things of the world, partying, clubbing etc. Those were the things that were familiar to him and as for me, I drew closer to my familiarities which was the church. I was at the church for every service they had trying to fill that void.

We soon realized that we weren't a compatible match any longer, however we stayed together because neither of us had anywhere to go. We both were hundreds of miles away from home and family, so we made do. 2007 rolled around and my son was getting so big. He was funny, smart, and really coming into his own little personality.

We were surviving, living life as best we could. Then in July I found out I was expecting once more. As tensions grew higher, arguing started to increase, and fights were breaking out. This was due to two hurting young adults with the inability to effectively communicate their feelings. This toxic behavior resulted in us splitting up once he told me "Those are your kids, I am done." I moved back to Louisiana with my family and he moved to another state.

I ran to God and I prayed like I never had before. I had developed a relationship with God so strong that graphene couldn't touch it. Here I was, having no job, no place of my own, no car. What else could I do but pray and cry and cry and pray. One day in prayer God said "Get up girl, remember who you are! You are my daughter and I am your Father." In spite of it all, I made it through. God gets the glory from this story.

Teara F. Stewart, was born and raised in the city of New Orleans. She is the owner/co-owner of multiple businesses as well as the Practice Manager of a dental office in Baton Rouge, LA. She is also one of the administrators and a member of the praise team at Tree of Life Christian Center of New Orleans, LA.

Teara is the wife to Louis and the mother to Michael, Malachi, and Caleb. She's a strong believer in the power of positive thinking in all aspects of your life.

"The mindset of the human being is one of the most powerful tools"

–Teara

16

The Baggage She Carried

"Confess your faults one from another and pray one for another that ye may be healed. The effectual fervent prayer of a righteous man availeth much." James 5:16

Sometimes in life, circumstances happen and cause you to question it. The first step to life is accepting the good and the bad. I remember when I was nineteen, I met this guy and fell head over heels for him, but everything you think is good isn't always good. See, he was a guy who every girl wanted, and I was lucky to have him.

He was charming but if I could say anything about this guy it would be that he loved jail more than he loved me and his freedom. The whole three years we were together, he was in and out of jail. The last time he went it was different because he was facing twenty year plus. To make matters worse, I found out that I was eight weeks pregnant.

So now I'm pregnant with no job, on the verge of having to return home with my parents and had a man in jail. Many thoughts were going through my head, like "Who wants to raise a child with a man who can't stay out of jail?" After weeks of going back and forth with him about the situation, I made the choice at ten weeks to terminate the pregnancy.

I thought it would be best. I felt as if a ton of breaks were lifted off my shoulders. This was one of the circumstances I had dealt with and no one knew about. Sometimes you have to make choices for yourself even though it hurts. Obedience to God and his word will save you a lot of pain. I was very disobedient to God and his word, so I had to go through unnecessary pain. Not obeying will teach you some very hard lessons.

By age twenty-two, I was living my best life, had a good job, my own place, and a car. All I knew was work and partying seven days a week. It was all going so good and life happened again. I remember it like it was yesterday, September of 2009 my cousin introduced me to this guy, and we hit it off instantly. We went from dating in a relationship to living together. Within nine months, we were living together in Jackson, MS. It was the best year of my life.

A year in a half after us being together, he asked me to be his wife. That was the best day of my life. Once again, the devil showed up. On March 23, my life was turned upside down and it seemed like I was in a nightmare and couldn't wake up from it. I received a disturbing call saying, "Mack had been killed." I was devastated and lost. Instantly I began to question God, "Why me? How can you be letting this happen to me?"

I felt as if my life was over. Was God punishing me for my past? After laying him to rest, my mom and aunt felt it was best for me to move back home. I was heartbroken, confused, depressed and suicidal. Many

nights I couldn't sleep, all I could do was cry and think of ways to be with him. I felt like I really didn't have anything else to live for at this point.

This went on for months and days. All I wanted was to have one last chance with Mack to tell him I love him, because on March 23, I didn't get the chance to hug or kiss him and let him know I love him. That chance was taken away in a blink of an eye. At this point I felt like life wasn't fair! Days passed and I continued to question God as to why, just why?

Six months had passed including our wedding day, and on this one day something came over me and I did something I had never did- dropped to my knees and began to pray, hard as I could. I never needed God as much as I did that day. I remember crying to God, asking for un- derstanding, peace, forgiveness, and more. See there's power in Jesus' name. I cried and called his name for hours.

Psalms 30:2 says, "Hear, O Lord and have mercy upon me Lord, be thou my helper."

On that very same night, I had a special visitor, Mack, came to me and told me it was time to let him go, he was safe with the Lord and would always be with me. The Lord sent him to give me the peace and understanding I was asking for, and as hard as it was to let go, I had to because this was what I asked God for.

Proverbs 3:5 "Trust in the Lord with all thine heart and lean not unto thine own understand."

The Lord and Mack gave me understanding and comfort to continue to live without him. I learned to trust God and to never ever question his plan. Always remember that God will never put you in a situation that He can't bring you from. I want to encourage readers who are dealing with secrets, life circumstances, depression, or suicidal thoughts to seek God first then professional help.

Don't worry about what people think or say about you. People will judge and talk whether you are doing something good or bad. See, what I love about my God is He was patient with me no matter how much I disobeyed His word or didn't follow His plan. He allowed me to go through these tests because he knew they would end up being my testimony.

There is absolutely nothing in life you can go through and not come out of. Always appreciate every opportunity God gives with people you love, big or small, because you never know the day, time, or hour when they will return home with the man above.

Maryetta Batiste, is a thirty-three-year old, first-time author, and speaker in the making. She is a native of Oakvale, MS. Maryetta is an entrepreneur. She's a supervisor at Caring Hands Personal Care in Prentiss, MS. who desires to help women see their true potential and deal with life's circumstances.

Through her struggles and hardships, she has made it her business to help others. Maryetta hopes her story helps other women face their fears no matter who may judge them. Maryetta wants readers to know how they view their lives will determine how they live it! Feel free to follow her social media or contact her via email.

Facebook: Maryetta Batiste
Instagram: maryetta.batiste
Email: maryettaarmstrong@yahoo.com

17

Forever A B.I.T.C.H
(Beautiful Individual in
Total Control of Herself)

Coming from a small city by the name of Springfield, MA, I grew up in a two-parent household to a working-class family who did their best to provide the best life for my siblings and me. My father had two jobs in the education field and a side job doing many odd jobs to make extra income. My mother worked in the health field in mostly management roles.

Although I lived in an urban community in the inner city, my parents made sure I stayed out of trouble by sending me to school in the suburbs which offered the best education. They also kept me busy with volunteering, sports, and church. Many people who knew of my family knew of the image that was portrayed, which was a picture-perfect family with hard working parents, raising children, and taking care of a sick child with cancer.

What they didn't know was while I had two loving parents, one of them was having their own personal struggles with what I know today as substance abuse, which would have an impact on my life forever. Most people have the image of what someone who has substance abuse might look like, from someone who is homeless to someone who may steal from you and sell your items. The truth is someone battling with substance abuse issues can look like a regular person and you may never even suspect what they're dealing with.

In fact, I grew up most of my life not even knowing what substance abuse looked like just like many other people. Yes, it was strange that my father had strange behavior, for example, the nights he was either high or intoxicated he would wake my brother and me, when he would get home in the early morning hours, and express how much he loved us and he would be very emotional and sometimes aggressive with his feelings.

My mom never knew my dad did this to us and we never told her because we just thought it was normal. I got used to my dad's behavior as just part of the "norm", even when he would go missing for days at a time. My mother never talked badly about my dad and they never argued in front of my siblings and me, her focus was on allowing me to be a child.

This went on for years through elementary, middle and high school. He ended up in and out of rehabilitation centers my entire life, but I wasn't aware of that growing up because my mother wanted to protect her children. My dad was very supportive and was present for most of my life, so it wasn't a problem for me until my dad stopped showing up for things that were important to me, like my sixteenth birthday or when he didn't show up to help move me to college.

When I helped my mom neatly pack all of my father's belongings and dropped the boxes in his car, I knew something wasn't right. Little did I know, my dad would have an impact on my life. Seeing my strong mother standing by my father would set the tone for what I knew to be the image of what a family looks like and the role of a woman in the household. The memories of my dad set up a tumultuous path for my dating life.

I knew of nothing but being strong and standing by men who had their own issues, which led to being in relationships with men who were emotionally abusive, men who were alcoholics and men who were caught up with their own image, but they had insecurities. This led to me having insecurities about who I was and led to me staying and enduring these toxic relationships because I didn't know that I didn't have to stay.

I looked at dating as something I could fix and overcome like my accomplishments in order to achieve the image of what society views as the "perfect family." I ended up shifting my focus and decided to build myself up to be the woman that no man could resist. While I was not so successful in dating, my achievements were flourishing.

I finished my Bachelor's Degree, joined the Army Reserves, completed my Masters, and landed a great career. I bought real estate, got a student pilot license, and was working on a great life for myself, but my dating life still seemed to be the one area I could not accomplish. I started trying to be the strong woman that I saw in my family. I soon asked my-self, "What's wrong with me?"

Those words stuck with me most of my life. When I began seeing a therapist and stopped listening to my close friends, who always seemed to wrongly advise me, I started understanding my behavior. All these years I was forcing relationships with people that emulated my father. The part I missed was standing by someone is not an indication of strength, but walking away is true strength.

I also realized society's image of what is considered a "successful family" is different for everyone and I am not a failure for having a different version. I am also thankful that my mother allowed me to live my life as a child and form my own opinion of my father, which allowed me to maintain a relationship with my dad even today.

While going through these dating experiences was not pleasant, I was able to grow from my experiences and become who I am today. My past indeed shaped me, but it did not define my future or create excuses to live my life with limits.

Moyah Wilson, lives in Washington, DC with her two dogs Virgil and Milan. She has been in acquisitions most of her career in the civilian and military sector. She also managed to achieve her student pilot license with the aspirations to become a commercial pilot.

Moyah decided to partake in her passion of writing by co-authoring in an anthology to encourage other women. She felt the need to write to encourage and uplift women not only based on her life experiences but based on stories shared with her by friends and other women she has met.

When she isn't writing, Moyah Wilson enjoys flying planes, watching sunsets, sporting events, museums, traveling and art.

You can find Moyah on social media at the following:
Facebook: Raeynette Wilson
Instagram: Ur_Lucky_Charm

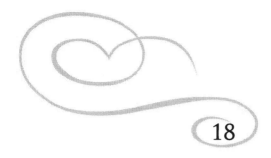

18

Daddy's Broken Little Girl
(Abandoned)

I'd been looking for love in all the wrong places. Sleeping with this one and that one, not remembering their names or even their faces. Trying to hide all the pain you have caused when you left me because you had flaws. I know you probably thought it was for the best, but daddy you don't understand years later you created a big ass mess.

You left me with no protection at all. I'm trying to figure out where the hell I belong. I know that God loves me, and He'll never leave me or treat me wrong, but why has it taken you so damn long to see how amazing, wonderful and beautiful I am!!! Your only daughter He gave you that was all in His plan!!! I thought you knew!!! When I look in the mirror all I see is you looking back at me!

I have eyes and ears just like you, but the funny part about it is that I have that little pug nose too!!!! People can say I'm not yours all they want too, but I look just like you. If they want to go a step farther DANA

(DNA) will tell them the truth!!! While everyone is worried about me, they need to worry why their father is questioning their paternity.

Old women in our neighborhood are always in other people's business, and they need to mind their own, while they're having babies for Tom, Dick, and Harry too. While their children are left fatherless, all alone, bitter and confused.

Their mothers are hurt, singing the blues. Daddy, what I can't understand is why you left me in the hands of another to be taught how to love, honor and respect myself and not to beat down and neglect myself. There were times at night I couldn't sleep. I was trying to figure out why my daddy left me.

Was it something I did that made my daddy stay gone for so long and never want to come home? Even though you apologized it still doesn't take away the fact I'm still traumatized. ---**a poem to my father**.

My mother and father split up when I was eighteen months old and I did know who my father was. We had a picture of him in our room and I asked my brother who is the man in the picture. He replied, "That's daddy."

You see I had other men in my life to help raise me; my other father, grandfather, my brothers, and uncles. These are strong men whom I love with all my heart, but they couldn't fill the void that was in my heart. As a young girl I couldn't understand why there wasn't a father figure in our home. We were happy; our mother made sure we had everything we needed.

She didn't miss a beat (not that I know of). But no one knew I suffered from my dad not being there because I suffered in silence until I became a teenager. It really made my soul dark and cold. I started to rebel, and I even flashed out on my biological father when he came home for Christmas one year. He only came home once a year.

I expressed to him how I felt all those years. How he took everything and the love I was supposed to get from him I never got. He was supposed to teach me how a man is supposed to treat me. I was looking for love from guys I guess that I never got from my father.

I would stay with men who would abuse me and misuse me. At a very young age, I started having sex and sneaking my boyfriend in my parent's house. I was thrown from a moving car by him because my childhood friend brought me a necklace for a gift. One night a couple of my friends and I went with a guy named Tom to his friend's house to play cards and started playing truth or dare.

We couldn't drive home so we had to stay at Jim's house. Jim told us we could sleep in his living room, but he had other plans. He told me that I would be ok to sleep in the room with his son. Later that night, he moved his son out to another room, and he came into the room with me. He then forced himself on me.

The next morning, he said it was consensual. It wasn't consensual. I was too drunk to make any decisions. I was scared! His wife found out about us and doubled back one night she thought I was with him and she had a gun. She told him she was going to kill both of us had she caught me there in her house.

Thank God I had a praying grandma and mother. That night I decided not to go with him. I just wanted to chill in my room. I was beaten nearly half to death, almost to the point of being unrecognizable by one of my children's fathers more than once. All of this because I thought these people loved me.

I started using drugs to try and cope with the void of what I thought was missing in my life. Years later, my older brother decided to have a conversation with me about forgiveness. He told me that everyone deserves a second chance and that I should consider giving our father another chance. I also learned that forgiveness is hard, but it's not for the other person it's for you- it sets you free.

Out of all of the failed relationships, I had three blessings to come out of all my mess. I joined the military, went to school, and became a phlebotomist. In the midst of all the bad, God allowed it to all turn out for my good. I became a better person. My father and I have a great relationship now and I owe it all to God!!!

Karen Dunomes, is forty-three year old single parent of three children, Tiyler Charleston, Lance Todd, Jr.,and Samoria Rayven. She attended Hammond High which she graduated from 1995. After graduation she attended Southeastern. After college, she joined the US Army.

After ETS out of the Military she attended Medical College in Baton Rouge and she was certified as a Phlebotomist. After attending Medical College, she attended Compass Career College to study the Medical Assistant program. Currently she works at XPO logistics.

She is a member of New Creation OMC of Hammond, LA Pastored by Apostle and Prophetess Jones.

You can keep up with Karen @Kae2sam on Instagram.

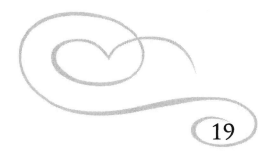

19

Letting Go...

We had not been speaking for almost a week. After being together for years, that was nothing new. People in relationships disagree and argue but this time it didn't even matter what I was mad about. You see, I had completely checked out of this relationship. I knew this was not how my life was supposed to be.

I knew being with him in this relationship was not my forever after. I just didn't know when or how, but I knew it would end and I would be free. Ironically, people who knew him were so charmed by the Dr. Jekyll side of the Mr. Hyde man I had been living with. No one had a clue....

I was literally going through the motions every day. I would get up, go to work, come home, take care of the children, cook, clean, and manage the house the way any good woman would. But, carrying out "wifely" duties and being a good woman was a duty and responsibility that he had dishonored and no longer deserved. On this day, I was keeping it as normal as I could, especially for my children. I retreated to the bedroom to watch television.

After days of us not speaking, he had now had enough. He decided that he was going to get my attention and I was going to talk to him one way or another. He entered the bedroom and began making disruptions, just like a child. I guess he figured negative attention is attention nonetheless. I didn't fall for it and decided I would be the bigger person, so I got up to leave the room. I never made it out the bedroom door.

In what seemed like one swooping motion, he managed to close the bedroom door, throw me on the bed, pin me down, straddle me, and wrap one of his neck ties around my neck. He was choking me. I could not breathe. I looked up at him and did not recognize who I saw. I tried grabbing the tie, but I was exerting more energy that I did not have because I could not breathe.

I decided the quickest way to get him off of me was to fake passing out, so I did. I closed my eyes, allowed my body to go limp, and held what little breath I had left. I must have scared him because he immediately jumped off of me. He shook me until what he thought was him reviving me. All I could think about was getting out of the house, but as a mother I could not leave my children. I was afraid.

He sat on the edge of the bed. I got up quickly to leave the room to get away from him until I could figure out what I was going to do next. I could not think straight. I walked past my oldest daughters' room. He was right behind me. Next thing I know, he hurled up all he had in him and spit in my face.

Yes, he spit in my face in front of my daughter. She was eleven years old at the time. I just remember her saying to him "What the hell is wrong with you?" I was completely out of my body. This was no longer the man I shared my life and my children with, but a thug on the street who had just attacked me.

I went to the bathroom to clean my face. When I looked in the mirror, I was so disgusted by what I saw. Who was I? What kind of example was I setting for my girls? What was I teaching them? I had stayed in this toxic, abusive relationship far too long.

All those years I was afraid to leave. While I said to myself that I deserved better, I really didn't believe it. I didn't have the courage to start over. I did not trust that God would see me through. That day was the day I let go.

I let go of the shame, the worry, and the fear. I let go of what I had internalized which was the idea that I was not worthy. I realized how much I had not loved myself by accepting to live this way. I knew I needed to set an example for my daughters. I would never want them to endure the trauma of what I had experienced.

I had to gain the strength, confidence, and faith to believe I was deserving and worthy of a better life and actually do better. Letting go of that relationship and believing my worthiness was me doing better. From that day forward, I began pouring so much love on myself. My "why" and my motivation was the love I have for my daughters.

I could not teach them to love themselves, train them on how they should be treated, and lead them by example of how to love themselves, if I did not first begin with loving myself. I sought counseling through a life coach and addressed the issues of my insecurities, self-doubt, and fears. I took the time to invest in myself. I discovered what I liked, what I enjoyed and what made me happy.

I made a list of all the things I wanted to do, places I wanted to go, and things I wanted to experience. I began chipping away at each thing. I created a self-care routine of morning affirmations, prayer/meditation, clean eating and exercise. I do all the things I enjoy like spending time with friends, volunteering, attending social events and traveling. They say energy is everything and "live your best life" is not just some catch phrase.

I have met some phenomenal people and created some amazing experiences since I've been on this self-love journey. It is evident that my life now is a reflection of how I feel about myself.

"If you lose someone but find yourself, you win."

Echo Muhammad, is a native of Chicago, Illinois. She attended Chicago Vocational H.S and would later obtain her Bachelor's degree in Business Management from National Louis University. She is co-founder of "Aspiring Black Women," a lifestyle company created to bring together a community of women to inspire, educate, and support each other in the development and maintenance of a healthy and positive lifestyle.

Echo is also a chartering member of the National Coalition of 100 Black Women, Chicago Metropolitan Chapter. She is a divorced mother of two daughters, both of whom are college educated and by far her greatest accomplishment to date. She is currently employed as a Project Manager for a packaging and display corporation.

Her passion, however, is international travel with fourteen countries visited and counting. She is a big proponent of self-development of the mind, body, spirit, and strengthening her connection to God to live her absolute best life and be the best person she can be.

Echo Muhammad
Email: msecho89@yahoo.com
Insta: @ top_shelf_e @abw.inc
Website: www.aspringblackwomen.com

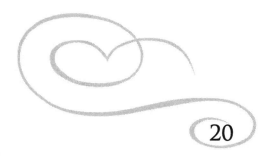

20

The Power of Release

Have you ever been in a room full of conservative people, whose posture speaks for itself? To the left you have these dignified individuals who have their noses tilted way to the ceiling, and on the right, you have a group of individuals that you know can't comprehend a word the speaker is saying.

You're sitting in the midst of these people with a girdle so tight, that all you can think about is getting home to release the pressure of holding all of that together. You're sitting down waiting to hear them call your name, but secretly crying about how bad your feet hurt because your heels are too tight. Not only are your feet going numb, but the button on your dress popped while hugging one of your neighbors.

The time seems to become longer and longer, and your concentration is now shifted on not tearing your dress. The moment you have worked so hard for is now becoming the most agonizing time of your life, and you are being robbed of an opportunity you may never experience again. My name is Royneisha, and this was my life.

I was officially crowned the queen of "faking it, until I made it." I knew how to maintain my status quo, while being broken and abused. Royneisha was never the type of woman to display her emotions and feelings visibly; no not me, but they were there. I was that girl they all called "Bougie", or "High Maintenance". What people never realized was, I was simply being "Me". Just like many of you, I experienced heartbreak, betrayal, failed relationships, and rejections.

At a young age, I learned my value and realized the power I possessed within. Growing up, my parents were absent off and on due to their own struggles, and what got me through was a simple prayer, "Lord, teach me to never become bitter and always have a heart to forgive." What I didn't know then, was every word I spoke was going to come back around to be tested. I grew up with a strong immunity to betrayal and rejection.

I became so numb to pain, that it was ignored, and it became normal. From relationships of being abused, to family rejections, as well as failed dreams and accomplishments, I became a "Cover Girl" reject. Beautiful white smile, long black eyelashes, and deep dimples. I had everything any ideal cover girl would have. The beauty! Take a moment and think about it.

In every magazine cover, the majority of what we see is a beautiful made up face. Every blemish, scar, and imperfection on their faces are hidden. I became that beautiful image. Because I had become the pillar of many people's lives, I adapted an identity that did not belong to me. I was so consumed with "fixing" other people that I was rejecting myself. I had an image to maintain, I had a position to fulfil, and I had children to protect.

Year after year, my heart was getting heavier and heavier. I have now become what some of you may know as the "Bag Lady". I was not your average bag lady. My Michael Kors and Louis Vuitton bags carried around manipulation, stagnation, unappreciation, and frustrations. I made pain look beautiful.

I could wear pain like a new color of lipstick, and wear rejection like a flashy pair of pearls. The compromised life that appeared to be normal, was now weighing my clutch bags down brick by brick. Life was like a hamster wheel that just kept spinning and spinning. That last blow was the final blow that sent a shocking signal through my whole entire being, which sent my heart into "cardiac arrest."

Every sense in my body has now been awakened and ready for battle. My very word on forgiveness was the antidote to resuscitate my heart and allow me to live again. Years of perfecting fabrication had run its course, and God has detoured the direction of my life. Just like the game Jenga, once you remove the block that isn't steady and strong enough to hold the tower together, the whole tower crumbles and falls.

Ladies and gentlemen, God allowed my tower to crumble and fall. I was a singer with no song to sing. Life had broken me into pieces, and I am now the epiphany of bitterness. Everything I worked so hard for has become an epic failure. Walking around carrying the burdens of others, battling with silent battles of rejection, had shattered, and broken every ounce of who I was.

I had become stagnated with where I was and accepted the fact that my life was centered around living for those around me who took me for granted, abused, and misused me. For months I waddled in my pain, gave up on my dreams, and isolated myself from the world. There were moments where I cried out to God all night, wanting to die from how I was done wrong. The suffering and pain was unbearable.

One night around 2:00am, I was lying in bed and I rolled to the floor and asked God to release this pain from me. As I began to cry out to God, I heard the Lord say, "I allowed you to feel the pain of every woman you will encounter on your journey." It was in my season of brokenness that I found healing and peace in God. I had to remember the power I possessed within, and that I was more than a conqueror.

I had to allow God to come in and make me all over again. God gave me a heart transplant because I released and denounced all the past pain. Despite all the pain I had been experiencing, the Lord allowed me to see it was "My Ashes That Made Me Beautiful", and you too can survive off of broken pieces. There's power in forgiveness, and there's healing in release. Get up, you got this girl!

Royneisha Pacheco, epitomizes integrity, sincerity, and compassion as a Certified Confidence Coach. She is a dedicated vessel, with a devotion to God, her husband, and children. A teacher at heart, Royneisha is a college graduate in Human Services with a mission to empower, equip, and execute.

She experienced a season of "brokenness," where she battled with feelings of rejection and betrayal. In this season, God gave Royneisha a supernatural "heart transplant," where God birthed "Beauteful Ashes," in which she is the CEO and Founder. Embracing her wounds, scars and imperfections,

Royneisha has dedicated her life to help women of substance embrace their past and to execute their destinies. Join the Beauteful Ashes society by visiting her website at www.Beautefulashes.com, and follow her on Facebook at CoachNeishaP.

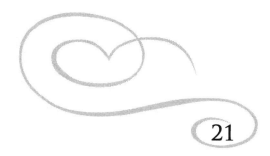

21

Redeemed Love

I was a slave for Jesus, and I loved it. I had just gotten baptized and moved to a different state. I was refreshed and excited about my new journey with God. Already being celibate for a year, I wasn't looking for anyone. One day, while out with a friend we ended up at the wrong location. Once leaving, our door was opened by someone who would eventually play a part in changing my life.

Initially, I had no interest, but his constant pursuit got me. Our first date turned into an adventure. That same night we planned a trip to the beach, and when we got there, he made me his girl. I got butterflies knowing it all was happening so fast. Immediately we were planning our wedding day and building a business together. I felt led in my spirit to ask him certain questions that didn't align with our fantasy.

As the red flags grew stronger, I was getting weaker in my Godly walk. I asked him a few questions like, "Were you ever married?" He answered, "No." I asked, "Have you ever hit a woman?" He quickly said, "No, never! Where are these questions coming from?" I believed him so I stopped asking. As I thought I was gaining, I was losing, losing myself, my esteem, my celibacy, and more.

I found myself obeying what he said not what my Heavenly Father told me. He was smooth with his words and slick with his actions. Subconsciously, I knew something was wrong, however consciously I wanted this tainted love. As time went on, the same marriage question came up. I got the same answer, aggressively. One night of intimacy twisted immediately and I felt my body being slammed against the wall with hands around my throat as I was gasping for air.

This can't be real, I thought to myself. I've invested so much time and effort into this relationship. I can't just leave now. Usually I would get "make up sex" with an apology attached, but I felt worse. Thinking things would get better, I ended up moving away from my rented room at my auntie's house.

I decided to be homeless with him instead to "build our business". I was so lost. We slept on my blow up mattress at the office, when my aunt had homes that she owned only an hour away. We would take showers at a friend's or his cousin's house or take bird baths at the office when everyone left. I did this because I loved him and thought he'd marry me.

His lies grew and although I was not serving God as much anymore, He still had my back. We got out of the car one day and a piece of his mail got stuck to my jacket. And guess what the mail said? Him and his baby mama's first name and his last. Yup, they were married the WHOLE time we were together, but I stayed.

He even tried to hit me with his car, and I still stayed. He'd occasionally spent nights at one of the ladies we worked with, whom he slept with prior to us starting a relationship. She would pick him up after every argument, but still, I stayed. He left me at an event, and she picked me up to take me home the next morning. Finding his hair in her bed, I stayed. When he broke up with me, I was led to fast from him for thirty days and on the thirtieth day, God told me to do ten more.

On my thirty-third day, I was working as a substitute teacher waiting for my kids to arrive. He then walks through the door as a substitute as well, when he had supposedly moved out of state. I took him back. When he left me for his baby mama and got an apartment with her, I ended up seeing a vision of her being pregnant. He later ended up finding out she got pregnant by someone else, and I took him back.

We decided to move out of state. We went to a job interview which instantly hired us. Having no peace, we went back to check out a room in a college apartment complex. While in a disagreement with him in his car, he socked me in the face a couple of times and pushed out his vehicle while in motion. I got up quickly so that I wouldn't be a victim to his craziness. My next thought was to leave, but go where?

I was stuck in a state where I'd never lived before and I didn't know anyone nearby. I went to the room praying he'd come back, and we could go home but instead I waited nine hours for him to come back bringing cold fries, chicken which I don't eat, and halfway apologizes. I had an exit plan which was to accept his apologies and act normal until I got back home.

As I drove eight hours back home, I felt off balance. Once I got home, I promised myself I'd never deal with him again, but part of me had other plans. I kept in contact with him and told myself if I just had sex with him one more time, I'll make a deal with God to send me my husband in exchange for being celibate until marriage.

I forced myself to have sex with him. I got back into church, cried, and prayed for weeks to God, letting Him know I wouldn't ever leave Him again. I bought myself a purity ring and prayed over it. I have been celibate for four and a half years now. It hasn't been easy, but it has been worth it. I've gained more of God's love and teachings on how to love myself and not depend on others for happiness.

Never receiving the love I craved as a child who suffered from many abuses connected to fear and rejection, God delivered me from it all. Now I am an author of an encouraging devotional for men and an owner of a tax business. God is so awesome. I wouldn't be able to do any of this if I didn't forgive and let God in.

Markasia LeBlanc, is an author, singer, songwriter, dancer, and actress. She speaks to the spirit of others through writing, using one of the gifts that the Lord has given her. She believes that using these gifts will help show others the light in Christ that they've been missing. She seeks to glorify her Heavenly Father in all that she does.

Social media: Facebook- Author Markasia LeBlanc

Instagram- Markasia_prays

Contact info: (909) 267- 6210

website: http://www.lulu.com/spotlight/Alettertomykings

22

The Girl That Got Away

I had been out of the dating game for a while, so I thought it would be nice to start talking to different guys because dating really isn't my strongest point. I was at a low point in my life where I did not know how or where I would be living in the next few months. I did not know how I was going to be able to manage a car note or rent, and my world just felt like it was going to fall apart.

In the middle of me trying to figure life out, I met Alan and we started texting and things were going great. We'd hang out from time to time and somehow it felt like life was really coming together. Little did I know that he was going to bring out the worst in me. When moving time came, Alan moved me into his home with no problem.

I told him what was going on and he without a doubt said, "Come with me, I'm not going to leave you in the streets." I was grateful but living with someone who I'd just met, and only known for a couple of weeks, made me fearful of what was to come. Living with a significant other felt like a mistake, but I had to suck it up.

Once we got comfortable with each other, Alan started doing stuff I didn't like. For instance, he would leave in the middle of the night and take my car. I'd wake up in the middle of the night feeling like a stranger in my home, not knowing if my car was safe because I was paying for my car. To make up for his actions, he would take me out on a date that consisted of either dinner or a movie.

The first couple of times it was ok because a girl must eat. It became repetitive and it got to the point where I did not want food or movies. I needed more than just a mini date for a cover up. I started to wonder if being together was healthy for both of us. Since we both used each other by this point, I felt like I was in a situation where we both benefited so why leave?

I got trapped into this "we help each other out" mindset that I lost myself. We both knew we had our faults, yet we wanted to be together. I wanted us to get our own place and I wanted to invest in the relationship we had created not realizing how toxic we were for each other. After a while, I dreaded being at home with Alan. He was always on his PlayStation or out.

If I was out, my phone was going off asking when I was going to come home because he needed my car. If I was visiting friends or family, they saw my frustration when I saw him calling me. It felt like I was never at peace and I could not enjoy my friends because I was so invested in this relationship that after a while it was not getting me anywhere. The only problem was I did not know when nor how to leave.

Months passed and late at night when I'd come home late from work, I'd sit and just talk to God about what was in store for me. I knew I didn't deserve the hell I was living in, but I did not know my way out either. Alan got an offer to move out of state and I thought in my mind this is the escape I needed. Of course, I was sad because I spent at least a year with Alan, but I knew this was the change I prayed for. Alan wanted me to move with him and I told him he was crazy.

He left and I knew my single life was starting over. I started working and going out with friends again. I started to focus on myself because I had lost touch with my feminine side. I started going to the gym and started doing things that relaxed me. I started to be happy with myself until I got the call. It had been a good two months living the single life and one day while at work my phone kept blowing up, it was Alan.

He told me he was back in town and that being away changed him, and he became a better man. I saw it as a trap and I did not want to fall back in that, so I wished him well. I told him I dealt with a lot while I was with him and I'm not going through that with him. I told him I gave him the opportunity to change and he rejected it, so now that I was out of a relationship, I just wanted to stay out.

I went out of town that weekend and spent time with family members and throughout that trip I realized that I did not have to be with someone who did not know how to value and respect me. I shed a tear because all I ever wanted was a significant other to appreciate me. Relationships are hard, and it's even harder when you are by yourself.

I do not have close family members that live around me, and I'm very private about my relationships because I don't like being judged for mistakes that I've made. For me, all relationships are a learning experience; this one I learned to take care of myself. I did not realize how important it is to take care of yourself. Always put yourself in first, second and third place. Men come in and out of your life, but as women, we must learn to be true to ourselves to be truly happy.

Gabriela Amador, is an American with Hispanic parents. People know her as "Gaby" when she isn't in a professional environment. She graduated with an Associates Degree in Journalism, and she's now launching her first story as an author.

While being a student at Delgado Community College, she wrote for the college's newspaper and some of her stories made the front page. Writing has always been a passion for her and while in school, she decided to write about different topics, gaining more writing experience. Some of the topics that she wrote included crime scenes, food reviews, and horoscopes for fun.

Gabriela can be reached at the following email: gabriela.amador713@gmail.com;
Instagram: gabs0713.

23

Life and Death within a Heartbeat

At the age of twenty-two, I became pregnant with my first child. The relationship I was in had just ended and it was best it stayed that way. We discussed my pregnancy, and both were excited to become co-parents, just not partners in a relationship. After my twenty-week ultra-sound appointment, I was told about the serious concerns regarding my pregnancy. I just remember crying uncontrollably on that day and many more days regarding my situation.

I was carrying a boy with "Potter Syndrome." All I could remember hearing was, "The kidneys are failing to develop," before I broke down. Without kidneys, there would be little to no chance of amniotic fluid and my child would have undeveloped lungs. With my grandmother by my side, I was asked if I wanted to terminate the pregnancy and if I did not want to terminate the pregnancy, I would be placed on a high risk watch, which meant appointments every two weeks for ultrasounds.

The doctor stated, in most cases, the pregnancy would terminate it-self, or I could complete the term and he could possibly be stillborn. I could not bear the thought of terminating my child, so I decided to see the pregnancy through. I was asked if I regret that choice and the answer to this day is still no.

With anxiety at an all time high now, I went through with the rest of my pregnancy, praying that some kind of a miracle would happen. I would spend hours researching all types of possibilities and share them with my doctor hoping that my baby could be saved. I've seen and heard of so many people in uncontrollable, unforeseen situations and God turned it around for them.

I was asking, begging, even pleading with God to turn this around for me. What I wanted for my life wasn't in line with the plan that God had for me. I just wanted to get away from the noise and the pressure of it all. I called and canceled my ultrasounds and took the bus to Atlanta. I needed my bestie and cousin to keep my mind off the pregnancy and they did.

Every now and then my son would bless me with a kick, and I would talk to him for a little while. I am forever grateful to them for that escape. After a month of my little sister begging me to come back, I returned home. Finally, the day came. I spoke to my unborn son and told him how bad I wished he could survive and how I needed him just as bad as he needed me.

I felt if my child lived, my life would be different; I would make a difference, I would matter. Little did I know that even in his death I would be different. My nerves had taken over, my mind was racing with a million questions, but I didn't say a word. I was hooked up to the machines for monitoring his heartbeat and my contractions, but they were muted and turned away from me.

I wanted to ask my child's grandmother what was on the screen, but I was afraid of the answer. I continued to sit in silence. The time had come. As I was being rolled into the cold delivery room, I looked over at the baby bed with the warmer and began to cry. The entire room began to tear up and reassured me that everything would be alright.

It was at that moment I knew that people didn't know what to say during situations like this. Even though it was words of comfort, we all knew everything wasn't alright. On February 23rd I gave birth to the most precious baby boy I had ever seen. There was no cry, just a small little gasp for air as I held him in my arms.

God, he was perfect to me. I held my son for the first and last time on that day. It is a moment that I will always be grateful for. To know that I gave birth to him but would leave the hospital without him in the car seat I brought, just in case there was a small chance of him coming home with me, still brings tears to my eyes.

Four days later we had the burial service. All of my family and friends came out to show love and support. I will never forget that. I remember feeling as if I was in a dream. Today I am in a much better head space. At times I still have unexpected tears, but time heals all. I have been blessed with four healthy beautiful children that keep me busy. We often visit the burial site of their brother.

"We are earth angels chosen to carry these special babies to Jesus."
– Anonymous

April Dillon, is a young writer from Hammond, LA. She is a mother of four beautiful children and is currently pursuing her second degree in Liberal Arts. She, along with her sister, Krystal, are currently working with known author, Deborah Collins, on a soon-to-be released memoir entailing the trials and tribulations surrounding their mother's upbringing that haunted them as a result.

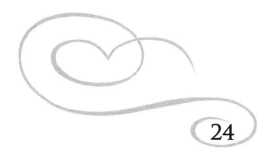

24

Smiling to Overcome Pain

It has often been said that a smile is one of the most beautiful things you can wear. However, some of the most beautiful smiles hide the most pain. Throughout my childhood/adolescence I have always had a jovial spirit along with a smile that could warm the hearts of every person I'd encounter. Little did I know, the smile used to bring comfort and reassurance to others, would later help me through some of the most difficult times in my life.

As a child, I had always dreamed of becoming a nurse but always had reservations about whether I would be able to complete such a difficult program. However, my parents reassured me that I could do anything I put my mind to. They would often quote Philippians 4:13 and that was the motivation I needed. I enrolled in the practical nursing program at North shore Technical Community College in May 2013.

A few years prior to me enrolling, my mother had been diagnosed with colorectal cancer. She had gone in for a routine colonoscopy in 2010 and a benign tumor was discovered. Sadly, a year later after having a CT scan performed, they later determined that the tumor had become malignant. The doctor suggested she begin treatment which consisted of chemotherapy and radiation. The tumor was the size of an apricot and was located on her lower sacral area.

Undergoing surgery to remove the tumor meant removing a piece of her tailbone, so her quality of life would be limited. So of course, my mother decided against the surgery. My mother began her treatment and I began nursing school on August 16, 2013. The first few months of school were overwhelming. However, I was able to find a balance physically and emotionally.

While in class one day in September 2013, I received a call that my dad was being rushed to the emergency room due to difficulty breathing. For years, my father had been battling health problems. My senior year in high school (2005), he experienced a stroke, which caused him to retire from cross country truck driving. Since then, he'd had so many health issues, but my father was a strong man. I often referred to him as my superman.

My father was admitted at North Oaks Hospital that day. After performing numerous tests, they found a large amount of fluid on his lungs and diagnosed him with end stage congestive heart failure. However. throughout his stay they attempted to remove the fluid but were unsuccessful. Upon discharge, he was placed on palliative care (hospice).

On December 28, 2013, I lost my father due to complications of end stage congestive heart failure. My heart shattered into a million pieces. That experience, along with being a first semester nursing student was absolutely life changing, but yet I remained steadfast. I pressed on, attending classes during the day, and caring for my mother in the evening. My grandmother would often help out, by taking my mother to doctor's appointments when I had a class.

During our fall break, I was able to accompany my mother to an appointment. Around this time, I'd noticed that my mom had been sleeping more than usual and complaining of pain more often. Surprisingly, at this particular appointment with her oncologist she refused treatment and insisted that she be placed on palliative care. My heart dropped and I was in disbelief. My mother was placed on palliative care and on September 5, 2014, my mom lost her battle with colorectal cancer.

Now here's where my faith was tested. It had only been eight months since my father passed. Here I am nearly three months away from completing nursing school and the two most important people, who not only inspired me but were my biggest supporters were gone. My world had been shaken. At that point in my life I could've given up and to be honest, the average person would've. Instead I persevered, showing up at class/clinical every day with a smile not once complaining and inspiring everyone I came in contact with.

Encouraging them to never give up regardless of what storms that may occur in their life. December 16, 2015 was my pinning ceremony, and my parents along with God, had the best seats in the church and my heart rejoiced! I truly believe that God put me through a test in order for me to come out with a beautiful testimony. So many people tell me "You don't look like what you've been through" but you see that's how wonderful God is.

He brought me through my storm without allowing depression to consume me. He kept all of the bitterness out of my heart and preserved me in beauty & peace. When I say "beauty" I'm not referring to my outer countenance but my spirit because I'm a true believer that some of the best blessings come from the worst situations and the brightest lights shine from the darkest places!

Isaiah 61:3 says, "To appoint to them that mourn in Zion, to give to them beauty for ashes, the oil of joy for mourning, the garment of praise for the spirit of heaviness; that they might be called trees of righteousness, the planting of the LORD, that he might be glorified."

The daily awareness of what God has done & is still doing for me strengthens my spirit on the inside and projects in my smile. Throughout life there will often be roadblocks that may cause delays. But for every roadblock you encounter, God will always provide a detour. Never allow certain situations that may arise, to permanently steal your joy. God's plan for your life is always thought about perfectly and for everything he allows there's a reason.

Beautiful diamonds are formed under tremendous amounts of pressure. In spite of how painful the process, trust it. Most importantly even on your worst day, never forget to greet it with optimism and always remember to smile.

Jaquella McGee, resides in Hammond, Louisiana. She is a graduate of Northshore Technical Community College, where she completed the Practical Nursing program. Jaquella is currently employed at Southeastern Louisiana University Health Center. She attends Sweet Home Missionary Baptist Church, located in Albany, Louisiana, where she is currently a member. Her passion for writing stems from insights she has gained from personal life experiences. Writing serves as an outlet for Jaquella, which not only allows her to express but inspire as well.

The authors of "In Spite of It All," would like to thank you for reading our book. If you enjoyed it, please do us a favor and leave a five-star review on Amazon.

If you or anyone you know has an idea for a book or an anthology project, please contact "The Writer's Block LLC.," and allow them to help bring your vision to pass.

They can be reached by visiting their website:
www.thewritersblockllc.com
or via email info@thewritersblockllc.com

Made in the USA
Columbia, SC
15 June 2020

11318405R00083